# Cases in Advertising Management

# Cases in Advertising Management

Larry D. Kelley and
Donald W. Jugenheimer

LONDON AND NEW YORK

First published 2009 by M.E. Sharpe

Published 2015 by Routledge
2 Park Square, Milton Park, Abingdon, Oxon OX14 4RN
711 Third Avenue, New York, NY 10017, USA

*Routledge is an imprint of the Taylor & Francis Group, an informa business*



**Library of Congress Cataloging-in-Publication Data**

Kelley, Larry D., 1955–
Cases in advertising management / by Larry D. Kelley and Donald W. Jugenheimer.
p. cm.
ISBN 978-0-7656-2261-7 (pbk. : alk. paper)
1. Advertising—Management—Case studies. I. Jugenheimer, Donald W. II. Title.

HF5823.K3443 2009
659.1—dc22 2008039868

ISBN 13: 9780765622617 (pbk)

# Contents


Preface ix

Introduction: How to Analyze a Case Study xi

**Part I. Advertising Management Fundamentals** 1

Case 1 Boswell Agency
Issue: *Structuring of an Advertising Agency* 5

Case 2 The Leaky Oil Company
Issue: *New Business Trade-off* 11

Case 3 Prime Media
Issue: *Global Expansion* 13

**Part II. Advertising Financial Matters** 15

Case 4 Tinsdale Agency
Issue: *Agency Profitability* 17

Case 5 Barrons Agency
Issue: *Agency Billing Procedures* 19

Case 6 Vineyard Agency
Issue: *New Business Profitability* 21

**Part III. Advertising Business Plans** 25

Case 7 St. Joseph Dispatch
Issue: *Advertising versus Editorial* 27

Case 8 American Textbook Company
Issue: *Outsourcing versus In-house* 31

**PART IV. ADVERTISING PLANNING** 35

Case 9 Phoenix Power Company
Issue: *Advertising Message Strategy* 37

Case 10 Go Organic Company
Issue: *Market Segmentation* 39

Case 11 Randall White Dog Food
Issue: *Advertising Planning* 43

**PART V. ADVERTISING BUDGET MANAGEMENT** 49

Case 12 Bosco Hot Sauce Company
Issue: *Budget Allocation Analysis* 53

Case 13 Alpha Airlines
Issue: *Budget Allocation Analysis* 55

Case 14 Southern Rice
Issue: *Advertising Spending* 57

**PART VI. ADVERTISING MANAGEMENT: DEALING WITH PEOPLE** 61

Case 15 Iportal Media Company
Issue: *Employee/Supervisor Review* 63

Case 16 Metropolitan Media Company
Issue: *Managing Upward* 65

Case 17 The Davis Group
Issue: *Hiring* 67

Case 18 JPT Agency
Issue: *Personnel Conflict* 71

**PART VII. ADVERTISING MANAGEMENT DECISIONS** 73

Case 19 Barrands Agency
Issue: *Advertising Spokesperson* 75

Case 20 Zeller Group
Issue: *Client Trade-off* 77

Case 21 Boston Life Insurance
Issue: *Advertising Strategy* 79

**PART VIII. ADVERTISING MANAGEMENT ENVIRONMENT** 85

Case 22 Zoomra Motorcycles
Issue: *Media Vendor Conflict* 87

Case 23 Glib Media
Issue: *Sales Incentives Ethics* 89

Case 24 Texsize Oil
Issue: *SEC Code Violation* 91

**PART IX. MANAGING THE FUTURE OF ADVERTISING** 93

Case 25 Arends Agency
Issue: *Agency Structure* 95

Case 26 Lawrenceville *Daily News*
Issue: *Forecasting* 99

Case 27 Thomson Media
Issue: *FCC Media Ownership Impact* 103

**PART X. MANAGING YOURSELF** 105

Case 28 State University
Issue: *Advertising Instruction Ethics* 107

Case 29 KMF Agency
Issue: *Ethical Issue of When to Change Jobs* 111

Case 30 Gotham Media
Issue: *New Job Responsibilities* 115

About the Authors 119

# Preface

Advertising is a fast-paced, dynamic field that is constantly changing. To be successful in the field of advertising, you will need a broad knowledge base, experience, and the ability to assess a problem and develop a cogent point of view quickly. *Cases in Advertising Management* is designed to help you gain this skill set.

Knowledge is based on information. Information is only as good as your application of it to solving a specific problem. The *Advertising Management* casebook provides a variety of advertising business situations. Through these cases you should gain a broad knowledge base of technical advertising skills, personnel management interaction, and business applications of running an advertising company. You will be asked to read, interpret, and apply your knowledge to solve real-world, real-work situations.

## Background

This casebook was developed to give students and practitioners in training programs a contemporary resource to guide their management training. The casebook is designed to be a companion to the *Advertising Management* textbook by Donald W. Jugenheimer and Larry D. Kelley. However, the management textbook was written so that it can be a stand-alone publication or be used with other advertising management texts on the market.

The casebook includes actual advertising cases and information (although in many instances the names of organizations and individuals have been changed). The cases reflect the changing nature of advertising that include a significant amount of digital media and integrated marketing communications situations.

## Organization

This book consists of many individual cases, each one dealing with a different area of advertising management. Each chapter is organized to include a case study as well as tips for interpreting the information. As with all case study textbooks, there is no right or wrong answer. You must assess each case and develop your point of view based on the information available. As long as you can explain and justify your decisions and recommendations, you can support your solutions.

As you go through this book, think about how to apply the information you are learning, how you might use it in your advertising career, and how you would use it to make decisions, explain those decisions, and justify your recommendations

## ACKNOWLEDGMENTS

The authors would like to thank the following for their help and support during the writing and editing of this book: Debbie Stanford and Debbie West, who worked diligently on putting this book into its final form and to the management of FKM, who provided much of the information and input into this project. We especially would like to thank our spouses and families for all their support, without which this project would not have been possible.

# Introduction

## *How to Analyze a Case Study*

The objective of the case method is very simple. It is to provide a framework for putting into practice what you are learning in the classroom. Case studies offer a realistic look at business situations and how you might solve them. Sometimes the answers are quite academic. Sometimes the answers go against everything that you have learned.

That is why the case method is so important. It is the one opportunity to make mistakes, take risks, and challenge conventional wisdom without fear of failure. Since each case is different, you must apply your knowledge and skill set to solve problems that are not always interrelated. This will raise your level of skills, and at the same time improve your proficiency at both written and oral communication.

The most important aspect of the case method is the experience it provides in thinking logically about different situations. The development of your analytical ability and your judgment is the most valuable and lasting benefit that comes from working with real-world cases.

Most cases in this book are drawn from experiences in real advertising firms. The names and locations may be disguised to protect the interests of the companies involved, but the overall situations are true. The final decisions are omitted, enabling you to reach your own conclusions without being forced to criticize the actions taken by others.

The case method is as close to real-world as possible. However, there is a big difference between real-world advertising management and this casebook. In a typical business situation, executives do not usually have the facts presented as neatly and clearly as they are here. Problem solving in the business world begins with extensive data collection, something that the cases have essentially done for you. Another big difference between the classroom and the boardroom is the time necessary to make the decisions. Here you read a case, ponder the problem, and develop a cogent response. In any business day, an executive may need to react to a problem immediately or within a limited time frame in order to optimize his or her solution. Finally, while your grade may be at stake in a class, an advertising executive may have client sales, relationships, or employees' livelihoods at stake within the context of his or her decisions. So, the stakes are much greater and the performance pressures more intensive at the business level.

That being said, the case method is, perhaps, the best and only way to simulate these conditions. It will certainly make you a much better advertising executive and a better, well-rounded person.

## Case Analysis Procedure

You can approach a case analysis in a wide variety of ways. For this case textbook, which focuses on advertising problems, we believe that the case analysis should follow a traditional business procedure. The following steps are the framework of any business white paper or detailed memorandum.

1. Purpose: Statement of problem
2. Background or situation analysis
3. Discussion of alternatives
4. Recommendation/rationale
5. Action plan or next steps
6. Contingency plan

This framework will aid in organizing your thoughts. Within the business world, this procedure may be too formal for many recommendations. Many business managers request that a one-page memorandum be the longest form of written document. In this case, the same procedure will work if you eliminate the discussion of alternatives and a contingency plan. Many times it helps if you can condense your thinking to a single page of text. That demonstrates that you have clearly thought out the position and are not using extraneous words or thoughts. However, for writing an analysis of a case study for a class project, this framework will be an excellent guideline for you.

## Purpose: Statement of Problem

Once you have read the case study and become familiar with the issues, you can then define the purpose of your analysis. It is good practice to assume that you are writing an analysis to a senior manager within your company. You have been given this project, and your analysis of the situation may help shape your career. To that end, it is crucial to clearly state the purpose of the analysis or to define the problem.

The following is an example of a purpose statement introducing an informational analysis:

> "The purpose of this memo is to provide an analysis and a recommended course of action based on the second quarter competitive advertising spending information."

This clearly states that you are providing an analysis of the competition and that based on this information, you will provide some course of action. Within the purpose, you don't need to state the course of action or the timetable associated with it. The initial statement is meant to tell the reader what the document is all about.

Alternately, the following is an example of a purpose statement that introduces the problem to be solved:

> "This provides an analysis and recommendation to blunt the recent competitive push of Dean's Beans into Bob's Baked Beans heartland markets."

This clearly states that Dean's is intruding on Bob's territory and we need to do something about it. Here the problem is clear. Any manager who would receive this document would be quick to read it and respond. The key to the purpose is to clearly articulate why you are providing this document to your manager and what will be the outcome. In each of the cases, the outcome will be some course of action based on the competition. Be succinct in your approach and use words that paint a clear picture of the issue at hand.

## BACKGROUND OR SITUATION ANALYSIS

The background or situation analysis provides the context for the problem. This is where you paint a picture of why there is a problem in the first place. In the case of advertising management, there are two overall areas that are typically addressed. The first area is external, which is client related. Advertising agencies are in the service business, and the client is at the forefront of their business. The second area is internal. The advertising agency business is a people business. An agency's assets, famously, go up and down the elevator every day. So, personnel issues are the other key area for advertising management to focus on. Let's take a look at each of these two areas and discuss some of the typical issues that you will be addressing within advertising management.

### EXTERNAL FACTORS OR CLIENT ISSUES

Advertising agency management and agency performance are closely tied to how a client's business is performing. If the client's business is good, there is love between the agency and client. If the business is not good, the client will put significant pressure on the advertising agency to fix the problem. Many advertising agencies have internal brand reviews where the account team briefs management on issues facing the client's business, so that management can head off any problems before they become critical.

For most advertising problems, there are four key areas to consider in a situation or background section of the document.

- Business and competition
- Environment
- Consumer trends and attitudes
- Communications strategy of brand and competition

Typically, these are the four major buckets that contain some form of problem. The initial one is the business or competition. The brand that you work on may have some business situation that has presented itself to you. This can be an internal challenge or an external challenge. Internally, you may consider the 4P's as a framework for the challenge. These are *product, price, place,* or *promotion.* There could be a change in the product, the pricing of the product, the distribution of the product, or the promotion of the product that has surfaced as a problem. Externally, a competitive brand may have changed something about its marketing efforts that is placing pressure on your brand.

The second major bucket is labeled the environment. Here we are talking about the economic environment as well as the overall business landscape. If the price of oil hits $150 a barrel, and gas prices go to $6.00 a gallon, you might see a significant decrease in your traffic if you are a restaurant. If we go to war, there is a negative consumer psychology that might dampen the consumer spirits. There could be legislation that might impact your brand. So, the environment is that myriad of outside influences that might impact your brand.

The third bucket holds consumer trends and attitudes. You may find that what once was a cool brand is now passé. Perhaps there is a new consumer attitude toward your brand that is impeding progress or making your brand less relevant. Perhaps there is an emerging market segment or key audience that should be considered for the brand. How the consumer views the world is a key area for marketers and can emerge as a problem area if not tracked and managed.

The fourth bucket contains the communications of the brand and of the competition. There are a number of components to consider. The first is the message itself. Is it relevant and unique? The second is the media mix and spending level. Is it on target and able to rise above the noise level? The third is the creative execution. Is it distinctive and compelling? Marketers are constantly fighting to carve out unique space in their communications. This is another key area in which advertising problems can arise.

The purpose of this section of the analysis is to discuss the most important facts that are the context to the problem. If the competition has changed creative strategy so that their message is similar to yours; then you should state what it is and how much you feel they are allocating to it. This is the area of the document where you are stating facts. This is not the area where you state hypotheses. Your goal is to give the reader the background necessary to assess your recommendation.

## Internal Factors or Personnel Issues

The second area that consumes considerable time for advertising agency management is personnel. Personnel are the largest cost on the agency balance sheet and they are the engine that creates the agency's product. Having the right people, keeping them motivated, and balancing talent cost with profit goals is a large part of the agency management role.

As in most service businesses, people in advertising present fundamental personnel issues. However, unlike most service businesses, the advertising agency is a collection of unique talents and personalities, so it requires a blend of special skill sets to keep it on course.

That being said, the typical internal issues of an advertising agency revolve around the following:

- Hiring/structure of agency
- Personnel appraisals/salary
- Manpower application

The initial bucket holds the elements of the staffing and the structure of the agency, which go hand in hand. Within this bucket is how the agency is organized today and how it might be organized tomorrow. With the rapidly changing nature of advertising from traditional media to digital media, an agency invests a great amount of time in how to structure itself and what types of talent it should seek. This is a key planning area for advertising agency management and has huge implications for the staff of the agency as well as the clients that the agency serves.

The second bucket is used to assess the current staff within the context of the agency structure. Since an advertising agency is a creative organization, personnel appraisal is vital to how the agency performs. Determining who is performing well and who isn't takes a lot of time and effort from management. Since people's livelihoods are on the line, it is a delicate area for management to address.

The third bucket for personnel contains manpower application: how the staff is used on various accounts within the agency. It is management's responsibility to ensure that the agency operates profitably. So, management reviews the profit and loss on every account in the agency to determine where there may be gaps or a misuse of manpower. The agency management must determine where it might invest disproportionately in an account in hopes of generating profit down the line.

All of these internal issues are intertwined. Who is hired, what their talents are, and how they are used within the agency—all these impact the accounts and agency profitability. And they ultimately impact the agency's reputation within the advertising community and its ability to generate new business to sustain itself.

From a case perspective, it is tempting to discuss personnel issues in more subjective ways. From a management perspective, it is important to initially treat personnel from an objective perspective since it is a business decision. Only after determining the best business decision, should management then determine if subjective criteria is more important than objective criteria. So, in using this casebook, keep the discussion in the background section of the case study to the facts.

## DISCUSSION OF ALTERNATIVES

Once you have written the background or situation analysis, your next step is to define possible alternatives to resolve the problem. Some of these may become obvious from the case itself. Others may emerge from your own background or further research into the topic.

Regardless of the origins of the alternatives, it is important not to generate an overwhelming number of alternatives for consideration. Management is not interested in wading through a litany of alternatives. They want to see that you have thought the problem through but not that you can generate a mind-numbing amount of ideas.

Typically three or, at the most, four alternatives are sufficient for discussion. One alternative should be to maintain the status quo, or to do nothing about the problem. There is always a tendency to change in reaction to the problem when sometimes doing what you have been doing can be the best course of action.

The discussion of alternatives is the heart of the case. First, you will want to succinctly list each of the alternatives in a sentence, so that management can clearly understand the course of action.

For example, if an issue is that a client's competitor has significantly increased its spending in advertising; you might consider the following alternatives:

- Monitor the situation and stay the course until you see evidence that brand sales are significantly eroding.
- Immediately increase spending to match the competitor.
- Test different spending levels to determine the optimum spend.

Management can clearly see that there are three paths to take. One is status quo, another is to become aggressive, and a third is to test a variety of strategies.

From these alternatives, you can then discuss the pros and cons, or advantages and disadvantages, of each. Sometimes it is helpful to actually make a list of pros and cons on a column within the case discussion. This makes it easy for management to quickly see what the risks or rewards are for each strategy that you have outlined.

## Recommendation/Rationale

Once you have analyzed the alternatives, you are ready to make a recommendation. This is the time to stand up and be counted. Either an external situation with a client's business or an internal personnel decision will have many "right" or "good" answers. But, this is not the time to be wishy-washy. A recommendation must be made with a strong persuasive argument, or your management will not believe in your recommendation. Many times, a passionately crafted wrong argument will trump a hedged argument.

This does not mean that you can concoct any argument and win, but it does mean that you must have some conviction about the direction you are proposing. The following is an example of a recommendation, with rationale, regarding how your brand responds to a competitor that has increased its spending:

"Based on the above analysis, we recommend that the brand immediately match our competitor's spending levels:

- If we don't match the levels now, we are in risk of losing distribution to the competitive brand.
- If we test different levels, it will be at least a year before we can read the results and by then, it may be too late to implement a broad based plan.

- Since our brand is in a stronger financial position than the competitor, by matching its spend we put a financial burden on the competitive brand.
- Our brand plans to take a price increase within the next quarter, which can offset the increased advertising spend."

A recommendation is a straightforward statement followed by bullet-pointed rationale points. Most managers look for at least three reasons why the recommendation is solid. Plus they want to see why this course of action is best among the alternatives you have just cited. In other words, you should be to the point on why the recommendation is the best course of action.

Some students may feel that they do not have enough information to make a decision. So they may recommend that you postpone a decision until you receive more information. This is unacceptable in the business world and it will be unacceptable in the case study world. Most business decisions are time sensitive. You never have enough information. But, you must make a decision to the best of your ability within the time frame that you are given. The same is true within the realm of case studies. They are simulations for the real world and should be treated with the same intensity that you would face the problem in real life.

## Action Plan or Next Steps

Once you have made a decision, now you have to implement it. Your next phase of the case write-up is the action plan or next steps. Here you will detail the necessary action to put your recommendation into motion.

Typically this involves a timeline of when things must happen, as well as a discussion of budget ramifications. You may also recommend how you will measure the actions that you have outlined. During this phase, if you feel that more research is necessary to get at the root of the problem, you can recommend it here. You may want to discuss any methodologies for measurement that you recommend, or any types of research necessary in this phase.

The key items for management are the time frame and the money involved. Those are the crucial items that a manager must approve. Managers are prone to action, so be sure to spell out the specifics of what you want to happen.

For example, here is an action plan based on the last recommendation regarding the increased spending for the brand:

"To implement this aggressive course of action requires the following next steps:

- Authorize incremental spending of $5 million for the balance of the year.
- Approve the media plan that details the incremental spending by 7/24.
- Upon approval of the plan, the incremental spending will begin on 8/24.
- We will measure the impact of the spending in the next wave of the AAU study on 11/2."

The action plan is very detailed. Put in specific money and dates. It is not acceptable to say something like the plan will be implemented within the next four weeks or that the money is around $5 million. Be very specific in your action plans or your management will feel that you are not buttoned up. If you feel that it is necessary to add a timeline or flowchart, that is certainly acceptable.

## CONTINGENCY

Even though your recommendation is well thought out and based on the facts at hand, unforeseen things can happen in the future to make you reconsider your course of action. Since the future does not always unfold in a tidy way, you may want to develop contingency plans based on potential outcomes or reactions to your plan. These can be based on a competitive reaction in the marketplace or economic conditions. They may be based on an emotional reaction from a personnel decision. Regardless of issue, it is good to have thought out the ramifications of the decision. This gives management a good sense of the risks of the outcome and how it might deal with them. Like the other elements of your analysis, the contingency plan need not be long—just simple statements in the vein of: If this happens, we would do that.

## SUMMARY

The case analysis is designed to give you the opportunity to solve real-world problems. It is a great method to teach critical thinking processes. As you move into the business world, you will find that your daily activities are a series of mini case studies. However, in the real world, they do not come as neatly packaged as the cases in this book. The case method is a training ground for making decisions with the data at hand. Remember, however, that the recommendations you make are worthless unless you can sell management on the validity of taking your course of action. But coupling the logical analysis with a passionate presentation is a winning combination in case studies, and in real life.

# Cases in Advertising Management

# Part I

# Advertising Management Fundamentals

**Case 1 Boswell Agency**
**Issue:** *Structuring of an Advertising Agency*

**Case 2 The Leaky Oil Company**
**Issue:** *New Business Trade-off*

**Case 3 Prime Media**
**Issue:** *Global Expansion*

The fundamentals of advertising management are similar to those practiced in running any other business. You have to bring people together for a common goal; organize your workplace, lead the charge, and always be looking to the future. Advertising is no different from other businesses in that respect.

Advertising differs from other businesses, however, in that it is a unique blend of people. So, while advertising is categorized as a professional services business, it is much different from the accounting or the legal profession, for instance. The closest profession to advertising is that of architecture where business and creative elements intersect. That is what makes advertising an unusual and exciting business. It also brings with it management challenges.

## Organizational Structure

Every business, including every advertising agency, has its own unique organization. There are advertising holding companies that manage a myriad of communications companies including advertising agencies, interactive agencies, public relations firms, consulting firms, and a wide variety of specialty companies. There are many advertising agencies that are privately held and there are many in-house advertising groups that service a specific organization.

In the advertising agency world, there are two major themes used in agency organization. The first is the *departmental organization.* This is where various advertising functions are grouped together in departments. For example, there may be a research department, media department, creative department, production department, and account management department. Work flows from one department to another.

In the department structure, the workers are specialists in a certain activity. Some are copywriters and work in the creative department. Others are media specialists who may be media planners or media buyers. In fact, large media agencies have a variety of specialists that include network television buyers, interactive buyers, and print buyers, among others. The advantage of the department structure is that many of the workers work on a variety of accounts. This helps the agency manage workload and it provides new types of work so that the agency team doesn't get stale.

The second type of organization is the *account team.* In this case, the agency is organized into small teams of specialists who work only on a single account or similar accounts. It is like having a small agency within the larger agency. Obviously, this is how the in-house agency is set up. The advantage of the account team setup is that teams become accustomed to working together and know the account very well. The downside is that work can ebb or flow and that the staff isn't exposed to other thinking.

The role of management is to establish the right structure for the organization. The goals are to make it productive in terms of its ability to do quality work, as well as to generate a reasonable profit. It is the management's duty to ensure that each of these goals is met and to properly balance the need for talent and workload with the necessity of being profitable.

## LEADERSHIP

In the advertising business, leadership opportunities occur in the management of most advertising functions. A good creative director, research director, or media director at an advertising agency must be a good leader. The role of the account manager is to be the leader of an account. Their entire role is that of being a leader.

One of the key roles in management is setting the tone or culture of the company. This is particularly true in advertising, where culture is one of the major differentiation points among agencies. Culture is the set of beliefs, practices, behaviors, and reactions to the business environment that differentiate one advertising firm from another.

Leadership in an advertising agency comes from all levels. However, there are key differences between the responsibilities of top management and departmental management. Senior management is tasked with leading the agency, setting agency policy, and working with—or for—both external and internal stakeholders. Depending upon the type of organization, senior management may be involved with a board of directors and stockholders, and also work with a variety of outside counsel including legal and accounting.

Department managers and supervisors are responsible for leading their departments from a personnel standpoint. This may include training, mentoring, and evaluating current and potential employees. This level is also responsible for administering the accounts that they work on in terms of their specific areas of responsibility. For example, the creative director is responsible for the creative product on the accounts that he or she supervises.

Leadership is a key quality required of any manager. The same is true in the advertising industry. Setting the tone and ensuring that all employees are doing their best to achieve success are vital aspects of advertising leadership.

## TRENDS

The advertising business is changing rapidly. It is nearly impossible to keep up with trends and new directions. Yet, one large part of management is to understand where the business is going so that you can be poised to capitalize on the changes.

There are three macro trends that are impacting the advertising industry.

1. The rapid movement to digital or interactive media
2. The move towards engagement—having a two-way conversation with the consumer.
3. The move towards globalization.

As an advertising agency manager, you must recognize these and other trends, and be prepared to deal with them. This may mean that you need to reevaluate your staffing needs in light of a change to more interactive media. Or it may mean that you must create an alliance with a foreign firm if you have only a domestic operation. Regardless of the decision, keeping abreast of trends and how they impact your business is another key aspect of management.

Obviously, economic trends are among the ones that management follows. If your agency has 60 percent of its income tied up in travel accounts and fuel costs significantly rise, this trend weakens the travel market, which in turn has a huge impact on your clients and ultimately your business.

Another key trend that management must focus on is the nature of the competition. If a new technique or service appears to be gaining prominence in the market, then it is management's role to decide if it needs to be integrated into the agency, and then figure out how to bring that about.

Keeping up with emerging trends is hard. As a manager, you want to keep up to date but not overreact to something that will prove to be the "flavor of the day."

In summary, the fundamentals of advertising management are the ones practiced in any sound business. Management must properly organize its workplace to get the best product, yet produce a sufficient return on investment. Management must set the tone for the business and provide the leadership necessary to deal with any workplace issues. Finally, management must take a long view of the business and be prepared to reposition the company based on emerging trends.

For more information on advertising management fundamentals, see Chapters 1, 2, and 3 of Jugenheimer and Kelley's *Advertising Management* textbook.

# Case 1 Boswell Agency

## Issue: *Structuring of an Advertising Agency*

Jill Williams arrived at DFW airport at 9 PM on Blue Sky Airlines from New York. The flight was on time.

"Thank goodness we came in on time," she thought. "I've got enough on my plate without having to discuss a flight delay when I meet Tom Bradley tomorrow."

Tom Bradley was the president of Blue Sky Airlines. He was a real no-nonsense figure who had many run-ins with labor unions in the past. He was a tough negotiator and an equally tough client. In fact, he was the largest client of Boswell Agency. Jill was being asked to head up the Dallas office of Boswell after being an executive with the agency's New York office. The president of the Dallas Boswell office had recently resigned and since Jill had prior airline experience with Continent Airlines, and had run the tourism group for Boswell's New York office, she was the choice to run Dallas. Naturally, this was stressful for her family. Her husband was an IBM salesman, so the move wouldn't disrupt his work. However, her son and daughter were both in high school, so they were not excited about relocating. Her daughter was especially distraught since she had recently performed at the New York City Ballet and was in a special performance arts school. They all liked the Manhattan lifestyle so Dallas seemed like a foreign country to them.

### Company

The Boswell Agency had grown out of Des Moines, Iowa, where it still maintains its accounting and financial activities. It began as an agricultural agency, but after its early success Charles Boswell went on an acquisition spree. He purchased agencies across the United States including New York, Los Angeles, Dallas, Atlanta, Chicago, and Boston. Through these acquisitions, he built the network of Boswell agencies that was now the twentieth largest in the United States.

This acquisition strategy brought many management challenges. Each office was largely independent and had its own financial goals. Although there were benefits to the network, it was not easy to get all the offices to work together. Power struggles and jealousies were a part of life.

Exhibit 1.1

**Boswell Agency: Dallas Office's Client Roster**

| Account | Billing (millions) | Total Office % Income |
|---|---|---|
| Blue Sky Airlines | 100.0 | 50% |
| Goodmark Foods | 30.0 | 15% |
| Oberon Printers | 22.0 | 11% |
| Bell Cellular | 18.0 | 9% |
| Roscoe's Sausages | 8.0 | 4% |
| Bluebonnet Cosmetics | 8.0 | 4% |
| Plains Bank | 6.0 | 3% |
| WPBA-TV | 4.0 | 2% |
| Singleman Auto Group | 4.0 | 2% |
| | $200.0 | 100% |

The Dallas office, which was recently headed by Peter Finch, was the largest in the Boswell system. It was driven by its largest account, Blue Sky Airlines. There was a rivalry between the New York and Dallas offices. New York had the second largest account in the system, Unimar Foods, and a variety of nationally marketed food brands. However, Blue Sky Airlines was a higher profile account than Unimar. This galled the New York office, which felt that it should be the hub of the network.

## DALLAS OFFICE

In her hotel room, Jill studied the Dallas office client roster. It was very telling. There was Blue Sky Airlines at the top of the list. It represented half the income of the office.

"It also represents more than 10 percent of Boswell's entire agency network income," thought Jill. "It's a monster," she sighed.

The rest of the accounts consisted of a variety of categories. Jill broke them into three overall areas. There were package goods brands such as Goodmark Foods and Roscoe's Sausages. There were high tech accounts such as Oberon Printers and Bell Cellular. There were local accounts such as Plains Bank, WPBA-TV, and Singleman Auto Group. The oddball was Bluebonnet Cosmetics, which was patterned after Mary Kay Cosmetics.

The local accounts had not grown significantly in years. But they were steady, and from what Jill had heard the agency had good relationships with the senior people in the organization. The packaged goods companies were also steady pluggers. There was not a lot of new product activity from either company, but they had to maintain support of their brands or be forced off the grocery shelf. The wild cards were the high tech accounts. Oberon had doubled in the last year and Bell Cellular was growing at a rapid rate as well. However, Jill knew that as quickly as high tech accounts go up, they can rapidly go down.

Then, of course, there was Blue Sky Airlines. Blue Sky was an aggressive advertiser. They were adding new routes and markets to their system. They had plans to expand internationally, which could add substantial growth to the account. Plus they had a strong business in commercial shipping. They were the only commercial airline to come close to competing with FedEx in this market.

They were very strong in shipping high tech components, since they had many flights from San Francisco to Dallas, New York, and Boston.

## Agency Structure

Jill then began to review the agency structure. Each office in the Boswell network was set up a bit differently. The only corporate functions impacting Dallas were financial controls, which were centralized in Des Moines, and network media, which was centralized in New York. Otherwise, each office had autonomy to set up its own structure as long as it met the corporate profit goals.

The Dallas office had never met the Boswell profit goals. This was largely due to Blue Sky, which took a sizable staff to manage all the aspects of their business. Since Blue Sky was so large, management had always been reluctant to cut back on staff or to ask for more fees to pay for the staff. The fact that Dallas didn't meet profit goals had always galled the New York office, including Jill.

On the surface, the Dallas office had a conventional agency structure. There was a financial group that reported to her as well as to the corporate CFO in Des Moines. The creative group was headed by Jim Clark, a funny man who always wore a Hawaiian shirt. He had a four creative directors and a number of writer/art director teams reporting to them. Jim personally wrote and directed the majority of Blue Sky's advertising. He left much of the rest of the work to the creative directors and rarely reviewed their work.

The media director was Sally Hogsmeade, a self-made woman, who began her career as a secretary and rose up through the ranks in media. She was noted as a hard-nosed negotiator but not as a deep strategic thinker. Sally ruled her group with an iron fist and had three group media directors who reported to her, and who oversaw the planning on the accounts. Then she had planner/buyers who did the planning and execution of the media. She set up a planner/buyer model largely due to the large local market activity of Blue Sky; the planner/buyers each had a number of markets that they were in charge of. They purchased all the media in those markets.

The production director was Richard Steele. Richard was a former New Yorker who had a print production background. He had a keen eye for design and worked well with the creative group. He had both print and broadcast production plus traffic reporting to him. He had also set up a business manager for the department to help him keep control of costs. The business manager was Emily Litrell. By most counts, she was the one who really ran the department.

The planning department was headed by Ian Howell. Ian was recruited to Boswell from Britain and was the first account planner in the office. He soon recruited a research person and a junior planner to help him. Ian was extremely gifted in developing insights and was a very valuable member of the team. His insights had led to the recent work on Blue Sky that had won industry awards. However, Ian often clashed with the creative department, since he felt that they should not be involved in overall strategy. Although the creative group respected his insights, they often felt that he went too far in leading the client into a certain type of execution before they got involved.

Exhibit 1.2 **Boswell Agency: Dallas Office's Agency Structure** (Conventional)

President

| | | | | | |
|---|---|---|---|---|---|
| CFO | CEO | Media Director | Production Director | Account Directors (4) | Planning |
| Accounting | Creative Directors | Group Media Directors | Print/ Broadcast | Account Supervisors | Planning |
| Billing/ Paying | Writers/ Art Directors | Planner/ Buyers | Production | Account Executive | Research |
| | | | Traffic | Asst. Account Executives | |
| | | | Business Manager | | |

Finally, there was the account group. There were four account directors. Hal Green ran the Blue Sky account. Hal was the former marketing director of Blue Sky and was a close friend of Tom Bradley. They had been college roommates. Boswell had been required to take on Hal as one of the conditions for gaining the North American account. It was an odd relationship, since Hal worked nearly as much from a client perspective as from the agency viewpoint. He ran the account like an in-house agency. Nearly all the key people on the account reported to him on a de facto basis, regardless of department.

The other three account directors managed the other business. Crystal Heep was only on Bluebonnet. Bob Pugh oversaw Goodmark, Bell Cellular, Roscoe's, and Plains Bank. Jennifer Meade oversaw Oberon, WPBA-TV, and Singleman Auto Group.

Jill didn't know much about this group. Bob was a relatively new hire from Chicago. Crystal and Jennifer had been with the agency for a number of years. Each of these account directors had a variety of supervisors, account executives, and assistants reporting to them.

## DECISIONS

Jill sat back on her hotel room bed and pondered. She had to make a number of decisions regarding how she serviced Blue Sky Airlines and how to structure the Dallas office to be more efficient. These goals seemed to be at odds with each other. She had heard of other agencies that had set up an "agency within an agency" concept. This meant that they set up a dedicated account group with all disciplines housed together to serve a single account. Boswell didn't have another mega-account like Blue Sky Airlines anywhere in the system, so she was not familiar with this approach first hand. However, she had friends at C+E, which handled General Motors and they had gone to that approach. She really needed to find out more about this.

On the other hand, an efficient agency structure should be able to handle any account, regardless of the size. If she set up a separate group just for Blue Sky she wondered if she was just perpetuating the domination of the account within the office. She had heard that the agency had not won as much new business as they should have, because they were known as the in-house Blue Sky agency.

She also thought about what she might offer to Tom Bradley of Blue Sky. He was a hard-edge guy and she must have a game plan ready for his account. Her head throbbed as she went to bed that night. Tomorrow, she must meet with Tom Bradley and then the staff. She then owed a preliminary report to corporate management within two weeks on her observations of the situation and what she would do to make the office better.

She thought about not only the structure of the organization but how she should come across as a leader. She had a very collaborative style in the New York office, but with strong personalities—such as Hal—she wondered if she should modify her style to be stronger and more aggressive.

The next few weeks were going to be long and stressful for Jill. She had to smooth the feathers of the agency's largest account, figure out a structure that would be more efficient, and demonstrate to the staff that she was a capable leader.

## QUESTIONS

1. How should Jill prioritize her agenda? What do you think should be her 90-day plan?
2. What questions should she ask of Tom Bradley, the head of Blue Sky Airlines, to assess the best course of action with this account?
3. What are the pros and cons of setting up a dedicated unit to service a single large account?
4. Should Jill change any of the reporting structures in the agency?
5. What steps should Jill take to make the agency more profitable?
6. What steps should Jill take to raise the level of the creative product of the agency?

Case 2

# The Leaky Oil Company

## ISSUE: *New Business Trade-off*

Last Friday, you, as president of your advertising agency, were invited to meet with the top marketing executives of a major oil company. They stressed to you the need for secrecy, and then told you that your agency was just one of three agencies that had been prescreened for this account review. The oil company was to embark on a public policy campaign as well as a branding campaign for their three thousand-store retail brand.

This was a very heady opportunity for your agency, which had suffered a loss of a major oil company through consolidation just two years ago. The marketing director of this prospective oil company went on to discuss the retail branding effort, which would be twice the level of spending of any other brand in the category. This was more than $40 million in advertising. That alone would be twice the size of any existing account in your agency.

Then the marketing director went on to discuss the need for a public policy campaign. He said that the company, which had been a joint venture between a U.S. company and a Venezuelan company, was now going to be majority owned by the Venezuelan government. Recently, the Venezuelan dictator had blasted U.S. energy policy and threatened to not sell oil to the United States.

The marketing director said that he and his U.S. counterparts would run the marketing but that the board of directors of the company would all be from Venezuela. While he assured you that there was a need for marketing, he indicated that he did not know how the tensions between the United States and Venezuela would ultimately play out. He also said that this information was strictly confidential. He had made a point of having all the agencies sign a NDA (non-disclosure agreement) so that if something was leaked to the press, his company would sue. "The Venezuelan government has very deep pockets," said the marketing director. That was a warning to not say a word on this sensitive topic.

Back at the office, you convened a meeting of your top executives representing each discipline. You described the situation to them and told them that it is highly confidential. If word leaked out, there would be significant penalties. You described that while this is an unusual situation, the size and magnitude of the account would greatly enhance the agency's profitability.

"We have always talked about landing the big one," you told the team.

"While there is some risk in this, it is unlikely that there will be another account of this size coming down the pike anytime soon," you added.

Not everyone shared your views on the account. A couple of the top executives were very put off that you would even consider this account given the political implications.

Judy Miller, the head of your public relations company said, "Can you imagine the fallout from our other clients if we take this on? Why, we will be called the anti-American agency."

You thought about this over the weekend and on Monday morning you are about to call the marketing director of the prospective oil company, when your administrative assistant tells you that three of your top executives want to see you now.

The spokesperson for the group, an old-line account manager, tells you that if you continue to pitch this account, they will leak the news of this to the press and will try to persuade the rest of the staff to quit. They also threaten to tell your other clients about the company that you might do business with.

What do you do?

## QUESTIONS

1. Do you decide to pitch the account or do you withdraw from the review?
2. If you decide to pitch the account, how do you deal with the disgruntled faction that doesn't want to pitch it?
3. Should you discuss this potential client with any other clients to gauge their reaction?
4. Should you seek legal counsel regarding the faction that is threatening to leak the news to the press?
5. If you decide not to pitch the account, do you retain the faction that is threatening you?

Case 3

# Prime Media

## Issue: *Global Expansion*

Bill Meade looked out his window and pondered: "The world is getting closer and closer today, yet our company is only looking at the United States." He turned back to his laptop and resumed his silent contemplation of the screen, shaking his head.

Bill was the CEO of the publicly traded Prime Media Corporation. Prime Media was one of the leading media companies in the United States. They had holdings in television stations, newspapers, and some magazines. They had been a real growth story in the early 1990s but lately the growth had stalled. The newspaper industry was shrinking and the magazine industry was not growing either. The television stations were in strong markets such as Denver, San Antonio, and Phoenix but that wasn't enough to offset the slower growth in the print division.

The Board of Directors of Prime Media wanted more growth out of the company. They were pushing Bill and his management team to consider moving into higher growth markets that were digital. While Bill agreed that digital media were a growth platform, he also believed that international growth should be considered.

On his desk, he fumbled for the article that had started his thinking. It was an economic trends article that detailed the GDP (gross domestic product) growth in various world economies. The forecast for the United States advertising growth was at 2.3 percent while other key industrial markets were running nearly twice that level—from Australia at 4.6 percent to Germany at 5.7 percent.

If these industrial nations weren't enough, there were also the emerging economies of China and India, which were rocketing along in double-digit growth. It seemed that anything that was in these markets was turning to gold. Through his media connections, he had friends in the governments of both Asian countries. Perhaps there was something that he could find that might be attractive for his company in these huge untapped markets.

He also had been approached by a group of German newspapers, who wanted to sell to a larger company. He had brushed them aside, since his board had made their feelings known that they were a U.S.-only company.

"What do we really know about the rest of the world," said one of the elder board members.

Exhibit 3.1

**Five-Year Advertising Outlook in Key Industrialized and Emerging Countries**

| Country | 5-Year AVG CAGR |
|---|---|
| Major Markets | |
| United States | 2.3 |
| Canada | 2.5 |
| Japan | 1.5 |
| Germany | 5.7 |
| United Kingdom | 3.0 |
| Australia | 4.6 |
| France | 3.0 |
| Emerging Markets | |
| China | 10.2 |
| India | 8.3 |
| Brazil | 6.5 |
| Mexico | 5.5 |

*Note*: CAGR = Compounded Annual Growth Rate

"There is plenty of growth in the U.S. before we go abroad," he added.

Bill continued to stare at his screen. There was a board meeting in a few weeks. He must pull together a presentation that would open their eyes to consider a broader range of growth opportunities.

He thought out loud, "How should I tackle this one?"

## QUESTIONS

1. Do you think that the information Bill Meade has is enough to go to the board of directors with?
2. What other information should he get to strengthen his case?
3. What are the other considerations for a company deciding between domestic and international growth?
4. Are there examples of other companies that have faced similar circumstances that Bill could use as support for his premise?

# Part II

# Advertising Financial Matters

**Case 4 Tinsdale Agency**
**Issue:** *Agency Profitability*

**Case 5 Barrons Agency**
**Issue:** *Agency Billing Procedures*

**Case 6 Vineyard Agency**
**Issue:** *New Business Profitability*

Every manager needs to know something about accounting and finance. And there's no exception in the advertising business. You may not need to know every detail or how to calculate financial ratios, but you must understand the basics of accounting and finance.

At a fundamental level, advertising is an expense that must be accounted for. It is also an aspect of a company's profit and loss, or P&L statement. A CEO of any company that is advertising will assess if the money he is investing in advertising could be better used to fund something else. Since advertising is an expense, it can impact a company's cash flow, the money that is readily available to make purchases or pay the bills.

Senior management in both advertisers and advertising agencies spend much time and attention understanding how advertising contributes to a company's profits on both a short-term and long-term basis. These types of financial analysis serve as the basis for how many advertising dollars are budgeted.

It is important that you have a firm grasp of the implications of the ways in which advertising dollars are impacting the company's financial position—regardless of the type of management position you are in, whether it be with the agency or the advertiser.

Accounting and finance are fundamentals in the daily operation of any business, since every business must generate a profit to stay in business. If you are an account manager at an advertising agency, you will have P&L responsibility on the specific account(s) you manage. This means that you will answer to senior management on how much profit your account is generating. In an advertising agency, the profit and loss on an account is a direct proportion of the amount of income an account generates compared to the man-hours put into it. If the account you manage is unprofitable, it might be due to a lack of efficiency on the account. Or you may need to ask the client for more money if you feel you aren't properly compensated. Regardless, it is up to you, the manager, to fix the problem so that the account becomes more profitable.

The hiring of personnel and how people apply their time—both have an impact on the profit potential of a business. As a manager, it is important to strike a balance between keeping costs down and providing the necessary resources to get the job done right. Many times this results in conflicts, since you may elect to sacrifice some profit potential to produce a higher quality product or provide better service.

Another aspect of accounting that is fundamental to business is the fiscal year. A fiscal year is the company's budget year. It may be a calendar year. It may be a July to June year or any other annual configuration. Regardless of the fiscal year, advertising dollars spent in a year are accounted for in that year. There are times when companies will allocate dollars in two fiscal years so that the financial impact in any given year is lessened. For example, if you are scheduling a large-scale production, the advertising company may ask you to begin production in one fiscal year and end it in another to amortize the expense into two fiscal years.

If you are a senior manager or head of an advertising agency, you will be responsible for the overall financial condition of the company. Your role may be to help guide financial policy, and this can include vacation time, health benefits, or sick leave, among other things. All of these items have a financial impact on the company. You will be responsible for how you treat your own cash. You may elect to use it to fund an acquisition or to reward stockholders or to save it as a cushion to ride out any down times.

The higher you get in a company's management structure, the more emphasis and responsibility you will have for making direct or indirect financial decisions. Your understanding of the basics of accounting and finance will be paramount in determining how much responsibility you will ultimately have in the organization.

For more information on advertising financial matters, see Chapters 4 and 5 of Jugenheimer and Kelley's *Advertising Management* textbook.

Case 4

# Tinsdale Agency

## ISSUE: *Agency Profitability*

As the president of Tinsdale Agency and Design, Lou Tinsdale had always been lax in his management approach. Perhaps it was his design background that made him a pretty laid-back manager. The creative capability of his graphics design firm had led to more advertising work. Soon, he found himself the president of one of the largest advertising agencies in Nashville.

Lou had just hired a new CFO, Bob Armstrong, who had a big agency pedigree. Bob had been with large agencies in New York and Chicago. He recently was with JWT until they closed their Nashville office after losing their largest account. Lou was excited to get someone of Bob's magnitude and hoped that Bob's influence would help the Tinsdale Agency become more sophisticated. However, he worried that Bob would not fit into the laid-back culture that he had cultivated.

That day, Bob had stormed into Lou's office waving a cost accounting report. Bob said, "Lou, this is crazy. Do you realize that we could be making at least 15 percent more money if everyone filled out their time sheets? We need to change this right now."

Bob went on to say that not everyone was keeping a time sheet. Camille and Jason, the receptionist and mailroom guy/runner, hadn't ever kept a time sheet. Jim, one of the old time copywriters was three months behind in his time sheet. Carol puts her travel time as a nonbillable agency expense. Yet, as Bob pointed out correctly, she is traveling on client business.

When Lou questioned why Camille and Jason needed to do time sheets, Bob was quick to point out that even though a high percentage of their time could be reported against the general office, there are times when they can legitimately report direct client time.

"Didn't both Camille and Jason deliver agency proofs to a client last week," questioned Bob indignantly. "That is an example of billable time," he added. Then Bob went on a tirade on how lax the agency was on keeping time. He said that was one of the reasons they were barely making a profit.

"You've got to stop giving away the farm," said Bob to Lou. Bob went on to outline a detailed plan to have everyone keep a time sheet by the quarter hour and have it done by every Monday. He also said that if they don't turn in their time sheets on time, he would withhold their paychecks.

"Let's make this agency into something," said Bob. He added, "I have no trouble being the bad guy on this. We need more discipline on this issue. Withholding their paychecks will send a message that we are serious."

Lou closed his door and began to think about what Bob had said. He wanted to be more sophisticated but he wanted to retain his culture. He needed to do something, but what?

## QUESTIONS

1. What should Lou do to ensure that his employees better keep track of their time?
2. Should every employee be required to record their time?
3. How should he distinguish between client billable and nonbillable time?
4. How should he treat travel time?
5. What should Lou do with chronically late time sheets?
6. How should he address the agency on this issue?

Case 5

# Barrons Agency

## Issue: *Agency Billing Procedures*

Julie Higby, the account executive on the High Plain Bank account, told you that her client was questioning the hourly rate charges on the account.

Julie said that the client knew some of the copywriters on the account personally and, as a result, he knew what their salaries were and had a good idea of how many hours they worked.

For example, Julie said that one of the junior copywriters on the business played tennis with the client and told him that he made $40,000 per year. The client then computed that if he worked 40 hours a week on the account he would have put in 2,080 hours per year. The client then divided the salary of $40,000 by 2,080 and came up with an hourly rate of $19.23. "But we bill out this copywriter at nearly $30.00 an hour before we apply our overhead factor to it," Julie reported.

Julie went on to say that the client feels that we are overcharging him by 50 percent. "He is hopping mad" she said.

As the CFO of Barrons Agency, this wasn't the first time that you had encountered this question. You were a bit surprised by it since you had gone over in detail how you bill out various people on the account with the client. Before Julie left, you discussed with her how the agency bills for their services.

"Here," you said, "let me give you an example with Jim, the junior copywriter on the High Plains account:

- Jim has a base salary of $40,000.
- We add an extra 30 percent to this base salary for FICA, insurance, state employment taxes, and other benefits. At his salary, that amounts to another $12,000.
- So, the total annual cost of Jim's services to the agency is $52,000."

"This total annual cost is then divided by the agency's normal annual base working hours. In our case this is 1,750 hours. Here is how we get to that number:

- We have a 37.5-hour workweek times 52 weeks in the year. That equals 1,950 hours.

- We then subtract from that amount our vacation, paid holidays, and sick leave allowance.
- In our case, we have two weeks of vacation or 75 hours, paid holidays that equal 68 hours, and sick leave allowance of 57 hours. That is a total of 200 hours.
- If you subtract 200 hours from the 1,950 total, you get 1,750 hours."

"So, that is why Jim's billable rate is nearly $30.00 an hour," you said in an even voice. Julie nodded and indicated that it made sense to her, but she had her doubts about the client.

"There are a couple of issues that the client is going to surface," she said.

She went on to say that last year Jim put over 2,000 hours of billable time on the account. The client is going to ask why the rate doesn't decrease if the hours increase. She also felt that the client would indicate that the 30 percent benefits should be included in the overhead charge that was also applied to the account. Right now the overhead factor was at 2.0. This meant that the hourly rate was multiplied by 2 when it was billed.

In this case, the overhead amounted to all the office services, including executive salaries that were amortized across all the accounts. It did not include individual salary or benefits. This was the standard practice in the advertising industry.

Before Julie left, she said, "Good luck in dealing with him. I know that he is going to try to lower the rate somehow."

As she left, you knew that you had to prepare to meet with the client and explain the billing procedures to him. High Plains Bank was an important account and you didn't want your integrity questioned. You sat down and began to prepare for the meeting.

## QUESTIONS

1. How do you deal with the client situation?
2. Should you consider changing the way your bill if you are challenged?
3. Should you bill more or less if a person works more hours than the normal work week on an account?
4. Should you confront the client and/or Jim regarding the discussion of confidential salary information?
5. How do you explain the need for keeping employees' benefits tied to their total billable hours?

# Case 6 Vineyard Agency

## ISSUE: *New Business Profitability*

Founded in 1990, the Vineyard Agency had emerged as one of the South's most successful advertising agencies. With a staff that totaled over two hundred people in 2001, the agency was seen as a creative powerhouse. All of this great work was based on the strategic thinking of Bill Vineyard, the founder of the firm.

In fact, the agency was a contender for "Agency of the Year," which was a prestigious award given out by *Advertising Age*. Bill Vineyard was a driven man and he built the agency on what he perceived to be a gap in the market. That gap was tourism. He focused on this sector and it served him well. He had won national accounts that represented airlines, tourism boards, hotels, and rental cars.

Bill Vineyard was a renowned speaker on the tourism circuit. He had everything going for him until the tragic events of September 11, 2001. Once 9/11 hit, the travel and tourism business tanked. Hotel and resort bookings moved to historic lows. Clients began to reduce spending and he began to reduce his staff.

The biggest blow to the agency came when his head account management person and his top creative team left to form their own agency. His creative product began to suffer and his usually reliable new business pipeline began to run dry. Normally Bill would get a call nearly every month to pitch a new piece of business. Now, the phone was silent. He needed to restart the agency and gain some momentum.

### ENTER THE NEW BUSINESS SAVIOR

Tony Wright was a slick New Yorker who had recently turned around two agencies in Manhattan. The most recent was Mariner, which he doubled in size within three years. They had just sold to WPP. After a transition period in the buyout, WPP dismissed Tony from the agency, saying that they wanted more of a traditional CEO. So, Tony was looking for a new adventure.

A New York-based recruiter called Bill Vineyard to introduce Tony's credentials to him. "If you want a proven new business rainmaker, this is your guy," said the recruiter to Bill.

Bill wondered why Tony would leave New York. He was a bit skeptical that a hard-

Exhibit 6.1

**Vineyard Agency: Income Statement (March)**

| Item | YTD Actual (000) | YTD Budget (000) | Prior Year (000) |
|---|---|---|---|
| Gross Income | | | |
| Production Commission | 162 | 200 | 117 |
| Media Commission | 893 | 738 | 550 |
| Fees | 36 | 36 | 32 |
| Total Gross Income | 1,091 | 1,174 | 699 |
| Loss of Revenue | 786 | 809 | 387 |
| Gross Profit | 305 | 365 | 312 |
| Operating Expenses | | | |
| Salaries | 170 | 150 | 130 |
| Rent | 19 | 19 | 19 |
| Travel | 3 | 3 | 2 |
| Entertainment | 15 | 2 | 1 |
| Computer, Phone | 3 | 3 | 3 |
| Legal | 5 | 2 | 1 |
| Depreciation | 6 | 6 | 6 |
| New Business | 16 | 12 | 11 |
| Misc. | 1 | 1 | 1 |
| Total Expenses | 238 | 198 | 174 |
| Other Income Interest | 5 | 5 | 3 |
| Net Income Before Extra Items | 72 | 172 | 141 |
| Agency Write-off | 20 | — | — |
| Net Income | 52 | 172 | 141 |

charging New Yorker would like the slower pace of the South. But, the recruiter said that Tony was ready to leave New York and wanted to show the New Yorkers that he could energize an agency regardless of the location.

Tony and Bill met in a neutral setting of Washington, D.C. Although Bill was not comfortable with Tony, he recognized that Tony would be a new business machine.

"With my contacts, I will be able to double your business within a year," said Tony to Bill.

"All I ask is that you give me control of the new business process and some resources to get the job done. It takes some money to get some money," he added.

Bill was in no position to say no. He needed new business and here was a proven big league new business guru. He thought that it was best for the business if he hired him, whether he liked his style or not. So, Bill hired Tony, who immediately went to work.

## FINANCIAL IMPACT OF TONY WRIGHT

As Bill and his CFO looked over the March income statement, Bill began to see the impact that Tony Wright was making on his organization.

On the positive side, Tony had been a great new business guy. Gross income was up by over 50 percent from a year ago. Tony had brought in different accounts from the ones the agency traditionally had handled. Instead of just tourism-related accounts, Tony had expanded the list to include luxury retail accounts and even some upper-end package goods accounts. This had certainly been a breath of fresh air to the agency. Even *Advertising Age* was giving the agency kudos for new business.

However, to get this new business, Bill and his CFO had budgeted for greater expenses. There were increased salaries to add more creative staff to the fold and there was a significantly larger amount of money devoted to new business. While the March numbers were a bit higher than they had budgeted, Bill wasn't too worried about it.

"We need the creative horsepower to get more business and we should be increasing our expenditures on new business," he told his CFO.

"I understand that, Bill, but I do worry that the new business Tony is picking up has a lower margin than our current accounts," said the CFO.

However, the numbers that concerned the CFO were not the salaries or the new business expense. The CFO pointed out the extremely high entertainment number.

"Tony's entertainment number is higher in one quarter than we have had in the last three years combined," said the CFO to Bill. He went on to say that at this rate, the agency would spend a huge amount on entertainment.

"Is this guy just buying accounts?" questioned his CFO.

The other number that the CFO brought to Bill's attention was the agency write-offs. The agency had been very good about not writing off any items in the past. They had made their fair share of mistakes but rarely did they have to eat any outstanding costs. Now, they had write-offs that they had never seen before.

"Bill, you must find out what is behind these write-offs," said the CFO. He went on to say that this type of write-off level was just unacceptable.

"Bill, I know that we need new business, but while we have increased our top line income, our bottom line is less than half that of last year," said the CFO. The CFO voiced more concerns about the bottom line of the company. He was concerned that all the focus on the new business efforts was not going to help the overall financial health of the agency.

## BILL'S DECISIONS

After meeting with the CFO, Bill walked back slowly to his office. His mind was racing. On the one side, he knew that hiring Tony Wright had been a gamble. But, the gamble seemed to be paying off with the rapid growth of new business. The agency was getting mentioned again in the trade publications as a "hot shop" and the people in the office were much more excited about the work.

On the other hand, he shared some of his CFO's concerns over Tony's lack of controls over spending. He wasn't sure if all the entertaining that Tony did was necessary. He had heard that Tony lived an extravagant lifestyle but he had hoped that this was just a Manhattan circumstance that would go away after he moved to the South.

The one thing that he couldn't overlook was the large agency write-offs. That was just like flushing money down the drain.

Bill also thought about the different accounts that Tony was bringing in. If they have a lower margin, he wondered if they were really worth it.

Bill had a number of decisions to make about the agency's future.

- Should he continue on this course with Tony Wright or not?
- Should he require that Tony get a certain margin on the new accounts or not take them?
- Should he rein in Tony's entertainment expenses?
- Should he penalize those involved in the write-offs to set an example for the rest of the staff?

Bill wanted his CFO to take another pass at giving him an analysis of the March income statement so that he could better understand the relationship of the top line income and the bottom line. He hoped that by getting a bit more detail he could better understand what he should do.

He closed his door and hoped that he had made a good decision by bringing in Tony Wright. The consequences of changing again were not appealing.

## QUESTIONS

1. Look at each question that Bill identified. What are the pros and cons of each possibility?
2. What further questions would you ask yourself?
3. How would you pursue each of the above questions?
4. What types of analysis would you do to get a better handle on the financial picture of the agency?
5. Do you feel that the short-term expense is worth it in the long term for the agency?
6. What would you do to solve the problem?

# Part III

# Advertising Business Plans

**Case 7 St. Joseph Dispatch**
**Issue:** *Advertising versus Editorial*

**Case 8 American Textbook Company**
**Issue:** *Outsourcing versus In-house*

Every business requires some form of planning. Managing an advertising agency or media company, or being an advertising manager for a company, all require some form of ongoing business planning.

Business planning requires both a short-term view, or goal setting, and a longer-term view, or objective setting. Business planning asks the manager to think about what success looks like for the organization.

In setting goals and objectives for an organization, a manager has three fundamental questions to answer.

## 1. Where Are We Going?

This involves setting specific goals and objectives that are measurable, and ensuring that the all of the manager's stakeholders understand and buy into the direction.

## 2. What Is the Environment?

Another way of saying this is: What are the barriers that we might encounter in achieving our objectives? The environment can refer to internal or external factors.

Internally, the focus may be on the company itself. Is the company prepared to meet the goals? Do you have the resources necessary to do the job? Will senior management support your goals? These are typical internal issues or possible constraints.

Externally, there are competitive pressures, economic forces, outside vendors or partners. All of these external environment factors can impact your ability to achieve success.

## 3. How Do We Get There?

Once you know where you want to go and have surveyed the environment, your final step is to prepare a plan to meet your goals and objectives. The trick in how you get there is to balance short-term goals with achieving the long-term objectives.

Business plans contain two overall sets of goals and objectives. The first makes some form of revenue forecast. The second states what type of organization you want to become.

All businesses must forecast or project future revenue. Revenue becomes the building block on which to develop your plan. There are many types of methods of forecasting revenue. The advertising agency business must rely on forecasts of income from current and sometimes potential clients. Forecasts can vary wildly depending upon the aggressive or conservative nature of management.

Advertising businesses must also decide what type of organization to build. This can reflect what types of skills you want to develop within your organization, which will impact the types of clients that you can attract and retain. Beyond the skill sets of the organization, management must decide what the company stands for. This involves what its corporate values are and what its culture and personality should be. In a highly creative business like advertising, setting the cultural tone for the company is as critical as properly forecasting revenue. The cultural aspect of an advertising company will greatly impact how attractive the firm is to both employees and clients.

Advertising business planning requires diligence and vision. While answering the three questions posed in this text may seem simple enough; great thought should be given to those answers. Business planning sets the stage for where the advertising firm will be in the future. With the great changes taking place in the advertising business, that is no small task.

For more information on advertising business planning, see Chapters 6 and 7 of Jugenheimer and Kelley's *Advertising Management* textbook.

# Case 7 St. Joseph Dispatch

## Issue: *Advertising versus Editorial*

Chuck Walker is a retail advertising account executive for the *St. Joseph Dispatch* metropolitan newspaper. Chuck was one of the top salesmen for the *St. Joseph Dispatch.* He had worked his way up from calling on "mom and pop" retailers to handling the automotive sector of the newspaper. This was the top-billing segment for the paper and was given only to the best salesperson.

Over the past year, Walker was able to grow the automotive sector by 20 percent. This was a huge accomplishment.

His approach to the automotive sector was to act like an advertising agency instead of a newspaper salesperson. He employed a combination of market research data and speculative creative to pitch the accounts on both the printed and online version of the newspaper. As a result, Walker had it rolling.

His prize account was Urbandale Motors. Urbandale was the newspaper's largest account. It was a mega-dealership that had a number of manufacturers ranging from General Motors to Toyota. Chip Urbandale was the owner of Urbandale Motors. He was a tough businessman but was also a true pillar of the community. He had donated much of his personal wealth to build a new library for the city as well as a new football stadium for the high school.

Mr. Urbandale loved Chuck Walker's aggressive style. He had been so pleased with the results of the *St. Joseph Dispatch*'s advertising program that he had personally written letters to the newspaper's management praising Chuck's efforts.

The publisher of the paper, Dick Heath, had circulated the letters to his management committee for review. Mr. Heath said that Urbandale Auto had relied heavily on local radio and television until Chuck Walker took over the account. By combining the newspaper's print product with its rapidly growing online presence, Chuck was able to take a significant share of the dollars from broadcast and turn it toward the newspaper.

"Chuck is one of the few salesmen that can help stem the tide of our sliding advertising sales," said Mr. Heath to his management committee.

## A NEW EDITOR ENTERS

To help ensure that the newspaper keep up with the times, Mr. Heath had hired a new editor, Dan Frank. Dan was particularly interested in being a consumer advocate. He had led investigative journalistic efforts at his previous paper, to take on many local businesses that he felt were duping consumers.

He felt so strongly about this cause that he had instructed his news department to set up an "action line" that appeared every day in the paper. The "action line" was staffed by seven reporters who led the charge to help consumers solve their problems.

After gathering information from the "action line," the reporters would call the business and get them to help the consumer. If the business didn't comply, they would list the problem and then name the consumer, store owner, and store name in the column much like a police report.

The feature had become very popular with the community. In fact, Dan Frank even had a two-minute feature on the local ABC television station to go over any juicy items. Most of the stories featured "shady" businesses and people trying to dupe the public. However, there were times when regular businesses were mentioned. This always led to tension between the advertising and editorial departments when advertising clients were cited.

Last month a segment of the "action line" dealt with a consumer's complaint at Urbandale Motors. The customer had purchased a new car at the dealership and three weeks later the engine block in the new car developed a serious crack in it. Despite repeated attempts to install a new block, the customer was still without his new car. The reason was that there was a strike at the producing factory that made getting the right engine block impossible. However, the complaint was given prominence on the "action line" with no mention of the strike at the producing plant. The "action line" screamed that Urbandale Motors was not responsive to the consumer.

Chip Urbandale was incensed at the "action line" item. Not only did they not cite the labor union strike that prevented the part from being shipped, no one had called him to ask his side of the story. Plus, Urbandale Motors had provided a demonstration new car to the customer at no charge until they could get the part from the factory to fix his car.

Chip called Chuck about the story and said that he thought that a follow up story or a retraction would be appropriate.

Chuck agreed and went to the editorial department to plead his case. But, no one would listen. When he got more aggressive about the poor job of reporting; the lead reporter for the "action line" said that he wasn't objective since it was his client that was in the "action line" item.

With nothing forthcoming from the newspaper, Chip Urbandale cancelled all of his advertising with the *St. Joseph Dispatch.* Mr. Urbandale told Chuck that he bore no personal ill feelings toward him but that he felt that he was mistreated. He added that he knows that advertising and editorial are two distinct departments but he felt like the journalism was irresponsible.

"I am going to put my money in the community newspapers that treat me right," he said. "I would love for you to work for them and handle my account," offered Mr. Urbandale.

Chuck Walker was dazed. All the hard work to develop the largest account in the history of the newspaper was gone in a moment. It wasn't just the commissions that he would lose but it was the loss of the relationship that really bothered him. Mr. Urbandale was a good man and he had helped him become even more successful through his savvy advertising recommendations. Now it was all for naught.

Chuck wasn't going let it go. The next morning he knocked on the publisher's door. He hoped that Mr. Heath would be a voice of reason in this mess. He hoped that Mr. Heath would not only get the account straightened out but would get more cooperation from the editorial group.

What should Mr. Heath do?

## QUESTIONS

1. What should be the policy regarding editorial items that impact an advertiser?
2. Should Mr. Heath print a retraction for Urbandale Motors?
3. Should Mr. Heath question the journalistic practices of the reporter for the "action line?"
4. Should Mr. Heath require that advertising and editorial meet regularly on features that impact the newspaper?
5. Should advertising be allowed to suggest news items or features for the newspaper?

Case 8

# American Textbook Company

## Issue: *Outsourcing versus In-house*

Founded in 1955, the American Textbook Company has grown and prospered. It is now one of the top college textbook publishers in the world. The company has sales of $200 million. It is the recognized publishing leader in many vertical markets including accounting, marketing and advertising, economics, and management. The sales of American Textbooks have always had a United States focus. However, in the past five years the sales mix of American Textbooks has changed from 97 percent U.S. to 70 percent U.S. and 30 percent international. The international market has become a rapidly growing aspect of the business. The other key change in the business has been the move from print to digital. E-books and e-commerce now account for 20 percent of the sales and rapidly growing.

The company has always done all of its own advertising through the use of an "in-house" advertising agency. The advertising department consists of an Advertising Manager, three copywriters, four art directors including an interactive art director, a media director who does traditional and online media placement, and two assistants who fill in various roles depending upon the departmental needs.

The advertising department is always busy. They write all the copy for mail brochures, letters, and direct mail pieces. And this is just the beginning. They've also done a variety of advertising including trade publication, trade show events, continuous updating of the Web site, and even search-engine marketing. Then, there is the annual catalog that they prepare for each division of the firm; it's always very large. So the volume of work is enormous. Just organizing over one thousand book titles for their promotional material and pricing changes alone is quite a task. The media person also has to maintain the entire database of 250,000 names of college and university teachers, bookstores, and individual book buyers.

## To Outsource or Not

Steve Carter, the new Vice President of Marketing for American Textbook, came from Meredith Publishing where they used both an in-house agency and a variety of advertising agencies to handle each of their divisions.

Exhibit 8.1

**American Textbook Company: Advertising Budget**

| Item | $(000) |
|---|---|
| Tradeshows/Events | 1,000.0 |
| Media (Traditional/Online) | 1,500.0 |
| Catalogs | 500.0 |
| Direct Mail/Brochures | 1,500.0 |
| Net | 4,500.0 |

Exhibit 8.2

**American Textbook Company: Advertising Department Salaries**

| Title | # of People | Total Annual Salary |
|---|---|---|
| Ad Manager | 1 | $90,000 |
| Copywriters | 3 | $150,000 |
| Art Directors | 4 | $200,000 |
| Media Director | 1 | $65,000 |
| Assistants | 2 | $60,000 |
| Total | | $565,000 |

When Steve landed at American Textbook, he was surprised to find that the company had never used an outside resource. He felt that an outside agency could provide the best service in developing individual brand personalities for each division, as well as handle the ever-growing and more complex media situation. He also believed that an outside advertising agency would look at each division more objectively and spend its efforts making each one distinctive.

"It seems like we are being penny-wise and pound foolish to have just an in-house agency," Steve thought. He felt that all the work of the in-house group looked the same and he wondered whether they were really taking advantage of the media world's changing dynamics.

He understood that he would have to fund an advertising agency. He felt that the budget he spent on advertising would support a firm if he allowed them to take a 15 percent markup or commission on media and production.

He also believed that if he hired an advertising agency, he could reduce the current advertising department to a coordinator for the database and a person to update the Web site. He might or might not need a manager depending upon the strength of the outside advertising firm.

Jim Lavaca, the Advertising Manager, was vehemently opposed to this move. He was opposed to it for the following reasons:

- He felt that the agency fees would not be large enough to get the best talent of the agency working on the account.

- There was such a steady stream of materials that the job was very task-oriented, which isn't an agency's bread and butter.
- His team was seasoned, and knew what to do, and did it with as much style and grace as time allowed.

"Why should we spend more and get less from an agency," Jim said to Steve. He added that every time someone in the past had suggested hiring an agency, they had found that it wasn't cost effective.

He went on to say that very few advertising agencies were capable of producing "effective" advertising in short time periods. Plus the anticipated "start-up" time would be expensive and fraught with potential errors.

"If we miss a mailing or get behind, the division presidents will scream," cried Jim.

Finally, he said that the cost for using advertising agencies could be higher than expected. He said that most would charge a commission of 15 percent for media and 20 percent for production, plus they would charge at least $100 an hour for creative time.

Steve Carter listened to Jim Lavaca's arguments but wasn't convinced that keeping things in-house was the best course of action. He felt that Jim was just protecting his turf. While he didn't blame Jim for wanting to keep the status quo, he knew that he had been brought in to make a difference. He also knew that his boss, Bob Hebron, would listen to both Jim and himself on this issue. So, if he wanted to pursue this course of action, it had to be well thought out.

So, the question that would be posed by Mr. Hebron would be: "Keep the status quo or use an outside advertising firm? What do you believe is the best course of action for the American Textbook Company?"

## QUESTIONS

1. What criteria should the American Textbook Company use to assess if they need to use an outside advertising firm?
2. Are there other options that either Steve Carter or Jim Lavaca haven't considered?
3. Do you believe that the quality of the creative work is worth a premium price over an in-house agency?
4. Can you name some examples of effective in-house advertising departments?
5. Can you name some examples of advertisers moving from an in-house situation to an advertising agency?

# PART IV

# ADVERTISING PLANNING

**CASE 9** **PHOENIX POWER COMPANY**
ISSUE: *Advertising Message Strategy*

**CASE 10** **GO ORGANIC COMPANY**
ISSUE: *Market Segmentation*

**CASE 11** **RANDALL WHITE DOG FOOD**
ISSUE: *Advertising Planning*

Advertising planning must be viewed in a broader context of marketing. The decision to advertise is typically weighed within a company against other means of growing its business. As a CEO of a company, you can follow two paths to growth. One is to grow your existing business. The means to do that is by marketing. The second is to acquire other businesses. After that, marketing is still essential for further growth. So, marketing becomes a key aspect for any company.

Advertising is typically the catalyst for growth within the marketing mix. However, advertising is not the only tool in a marketer's arsenal. The 4Ps of marketing are:

- Price—Pricing of the product relative to others in the category.
- Place—Distribution of the product within a retail set or geographical area.
- Product—Positioning of the product and the attributes of the product.
- Promotion—Any form of promotion including public relations, sales promotion, and advertising.

A marketer must weigh each of these four areas in terms of how to grow a brand. Not only must you, as a marketer, weigh each of these elements but you must decide the interrelationship among them. For example, the quickest way to increase sales is to increase the price of the product, the first P. However, this assumes that consumers will pay more for the brand. Advertising can be used to strengthen the value of the brand within the consumer's mind. The same can be said for gaining distribution—place, the second P. If you open a new market and don't advertise your brand, it is likely that you will lose the distribution that you worked so hard to gain.

Obviously, advertising and the product are intertwined. How the product is positioned in the marketplace has a direct bearing on how one promotes or advertises it. Product positioning, the third P, typically dictates how a marketer segments the market. Segmentation is a key element in the advertising objectives or planning of an advertising campaign.

How the brand is integrated within the sales organization has ramifications on advertising planning. Advertising must support sales whether it is internal or external to the brand. When planning an advertising campaign, how the brand is actually sold plays a central role in how an advertising campaign is developed and executed.

The final P, or promotion, includes advertising as part of an integrated marketing communications (IMC) effort. Advertising may play the central role or it may be a supporting cast member in the IMC mix.

Advertising planning goes hand in hand with marketing planning. Good advertising planning works in concert with marketing planning so that it is aligned with the overall marketing goals and objectives.

Advertising planning also plays a role in product testing. Many brands test either new products or improvements to existing products through the use of concept testing. Concept testing is a method through which a marketer will develop a value proposition about the brand and test it with consumers. Advertising becomes a key aspect of this testing since communicating the value proposition falls squarely in the advertising arena.

To develop a proper advertising plan, you need to understand who you are marketing to, where you are marketing, when you are marketing. The advertising plan then becomes the how you will do it.

The "how you will do it," or the plan itself, shouldn't be executed in a vacuum. Any good advertising plan must take into account the competition and their plans. The competition along with other inside and outside environmental influences then become a part of a situation analysis or SWOT analysis (covering Strengths, Weaknesses, Opportunities, Threats); this forms a foundation for advertising planning.

In summary, advertising planning is a part of marketing planning. They must be aligned. Advertising planning must take into account all aspects of the brand from positioning to sales. To be effective in the marketplace, advertising planning should take into account any outside influences and provide a SWOT analysis as a foundation for planning.

For more information on advertising planning, please consult Chapters 8 and 9 in Jugenheimer and Kelley's *Advertising Management* textbook.

# Case 9 Phoenix Power Company

## ISSUE: *Advertising Message Strategy*

Phoenix Power's electric rates are among the highest in the country, a fact that is resented by many of the company's customer base.

In an attempt to overcome this negative public opinion, Phoenix Power had borrowed a technique that has proven to be effective for other energy marketers. This involved developing an advertising campaign that demonstrated how customers could save energy costs by using better insulation in their homes or by purchasing more energy efficient appliances, including air conditioners. By using all of these conservation methods, homeowners could save up to 20 percent on their cooling bill. In Phoenix, where the summer temperatures are continually above 100 degrees, that could be a substantial amount of money.

Now the company was applying for a rate increase to help offset the increased cost of doing business. The increase was largely due to the proposed building of a nuclear reactor in Arizona that would become a power source for the city of Phoenix. The new reactor was also controversial because many people in the state were concerned about having a nuclear plant close to them.

Regardless of the consumer sentiment, the legislature approved Phoenix Power's plans to build the nuclear reactor and will likely give the company permission for at least part, if not all, of the requested rate increase.

Once the nuclear power plant is built, Phoenix Power management believes that energy prices can be reduced, since the company will no longer have to import energy from power plants in California.

"Once the nuclear plant is built, Arizona will have a total in-state energy solution," said a Phoenix Power spokesperson.

Now Phoenix Power wants to develop a short-term advertising campaign to explain to customers why rates will be rising and to prepare customers for the anticipated rate increase.

What creative strategy can be used to help communicate this unpopular message to a very skeptical and unreceptive audience?

## QUESTIONS

1. Should Phoenix Power advertise at all or should it put its efforts into public relations to help tell its story?
2. If Phoenix Power does advertise, what medium do you believe would be the best at telling the story?
3. What type of creative execution do you believe would be the best approach?
4. What type of research might you consider before coming out with a campaign?

# Case 10 Go Organic Company

## Issue: *Market Segmentation*

Go Organic Foods, based in Omaha, Nebraska, is one of the newest package foods companies to jump on the organic bandwagon. Go Organic offers a variety of products that can be found in grocery stores, specialty health food stores, and even some restaurants and other food-service establishments.

One of the best-selling brands in their product line is Go Organic frozen food. This was the brainchild of founder Robert Sierra, who learned of a method called "flash frozen," where you can maintain all the nutrients in the food even though it is frozen. Mr. Sierra was tremendously excited about this process since he believed that it would solve a larger problem in America, that of obesity. Mr. Sierra had studied America's eating habits for years and realized that much of the country's diet consisted of high fat and sodium frozen food meals. In fact, Mr. Sierra had seen his own mother and father gain considerable weight and later develop heart disease as a result of poor dietary habits. All Mr. Sierra could remember was that their diet was driven by frozen food.

So, Mr. Sierra used this new technology to develop a line of frozen dinners that were low in fat, sodium, and cholesterol, and high in nutrients. Even with this seemingly large breakthrough, grocers were reluctant to carry the items. They didn't believe that there was a large consumer demand for natural or organic foods. They told Mr. Sierra that it was a niche item.

Undaunted, Mr. Sierra finally convinced the president of a small independent chain of high-quality stores to carry the product. Sales of the Go Organic dinners began to take hold. The flavor of Go Organic products exceeded expectation and soon those who wished to eat a low-fat, nutritious meal without sacrificing flavor were flocking to the brand. Retailers who had previously been reluctant to carry the brand began to call Go Organic.

Although men tend to eat frozen dinners more often than women, the Go Organic line of frozen dinners was aimed primarily at women over the age of forty. However, the company soon learned that men also liked the Go Organic dinners as well. This popularity spurred Go Organic to expand their product line to include more frozen dinners, some breakfast items, and even desserts.

Naturally, the competition in the frozen food category did not stand still while Go Organic captured market share. They also focused on health in their advertising, and soon introduced their own organic or part organic frozen food products. The frozen food marketplace was becoming an organic and natural foods battleground.

Carol Hart, the vice president of marketing for Go Organic, looked at the trends of the business with some trepidation. The competition had significant capital compared to the small, privately held, Go Organic. Carol was concerned about the growth of the brand and if they could keep up with the constant battle for market share.

While she was mulling things over, Mr. Sierra entered her office and tossed an article on her desk. He said that this article summed up the market segment that he felt was still untapped by his brand. He asked Carol to read the article and to provide him with a point of view on the best way to develop consumer segmentation for the brand.

## The Article Provided the Following Information

According to a recent government report, obesity among adults had doubled since 1980, while being overweight had tripled among adolescents. One study cited rates as high as 15 percent of teenage boys and girls being overweight.

Hispanics and African Americans had a much higher prevalence for being overweight than the Caucasian population. Women were more likely to be obese compared to men.

Mr. Sierra turned to Carol and said, "Look at these statistics. We need to rethink our market segmentation strategy. Why, homes that have teens and ethnic audiences are totally untapped markets for us. I would like a report on how we segment our future market within the next week."

As Mr. Sierra left, Carol felt very conflicted. She knew that he was passionate about wanting to help people who had a high proclivity for being obese, yet she was looking at other demographic information on frozen food purchasers and organic food buyers that was very different from this information.

Given the recent amount of competition in the marketplace, she knew that they had to be right in how they segmented the market. She began to quickly review the data and assemble a presentation. She hoped that she was right.

## Questions

1. Do you think that the information about segmentation is enough to develop a segmentation scheme for the brand?
2. Which information do you consider more valuable, the trends Carol was looking at or the facts in the article? Why?
3. What trends would you consider as you developed a segmentation strategy?
4. Do you feel that the segmentation strategy should be based on adding new purchasers to the brand or adding frequency to current buyers?
5. What would be the ideal information to have to make this decision?
6. Would you go with the information you have, or recommend that you take more time and do primary research on the market before making a decision?

Exhibit 10.1

**Information According to a Recent Government Report**

| Demographics | Frozen Dinner Consumption | Organic Food Consumption | Obesity Likelihood |
|---|---|---|---|
| Average Index | 100 | 100 | 100 |
| Gender | | | |
| Men | 110 | 50 | 80 |
| Women | 90 | 150 | 120 |
| Age | | | |
| Teens 13–17 | 65 | 20 | 120 |
| Adults 18–24 | 120 | 30 | 110 |
| 25–34 | 110 | 100 | 70 |
| 35–54 | 80 | 110 | 70 |
| 55–64 | 70 | 140 | 90 |
| 65+ | 130 | 60 | 120 |
| Ethnicity | | | |
| Caucasian | 100 | 130 | 70 |
| African American | 100 | 50 | 140 |
| Hispanic | 70 | 40 | 150 |
| Asian | 110 | 150 | 60 |
| Native American | 20 | 30 | 180 |
| Education | | | |
| High School or Less | 115 | 30 | 150 |
| High School Grad | 105 | 70 | 120 |
| Some College | 100 | 100 | 100 |
| College Grad | 95 | 130 | 75 |
| Grad School | 60 | 180 | 50 |
| Income | | | |
| $50k or Less | 100 | 40 | 150 |
| $50k to $100k | 120 | 80 | 110 |
| $100k or More | 90 | 170 | 60 |

*Note:* Index to Average is 100. Above 100 is more likely, below 100 is less likely.

Case 11

# Randall White Dog Food

Issue: *Advertising Planning*

The Randall White Feed and Milling Company is an old-line regional marketer of farm feeds, grits, and corn meal. It was established in 1929 in Berry, Georgia, by Robert White.

Berry, Georgia, has been dubbed the "bird dog capital of the world" by *Popular Hunting* magazine. Robert White was a hunting enthusiast. His favorite avocations were hunting quail and raising bird dogs. He and his son, Randall, had been recognized as a top father/son hunting duo by *Popular Hunting*.

Robert White soon turned his passion into profits. He used his money and the resources from his milling operation to develop and market a dry dog food formula specially made for hunting dogs. He named the brand after his son, Randall, and launched the Randall White Complete Dog Ration brand.

Today, Randall White Complete Dog Ration is the company's largest volume and highest profit margin product. It is also the number one brand of dog food in its limited distribution area.

## The Product

Randall White Complete Dog Ration is a high energy, high protein, complete and nutritionally balanced dry dog food in concentrated form. The brand has historically been positioned as a high performance dog food for dog owners who desire superior nutrition. This positioning was designed specifically for hunting dogs and for working farm dogs. It is a premium priced product and appeals to the hunting enthusiast and to dog owners who have large, active dogs.

## The Dog Food Market

The dry dog food market is big and growing fast. Sales for the last year nationally and in the Southeast (Randall White's marketing area) were both very strong.

From a distribution perspective, grocery stores are the dominant outlets; closely followed by pet food stores and by feed and farm implement stores. Randall White

Exhibit 11.1

**Dry Dog Food Sales and 5-Year CAGR**

| | Total Sales Millions $ | % CAGR |
|---|---|---|
| National | 2,000 | 8.6 |
| Southeast | 750 | 13.3 |

*Note*: CAGR = Compounded Annual Growth Rate

Exhibit 11.2

**Sales Distribution of Dry Dog Food Sales and Randall White Brand** (% Distribution)

| | Grocery | National Pet Stores | Farm/Feed | Kennels/Local |
|---|---|---|---|---|
| National | 55 | 30 | 5 | 10 |
| Southeast | 50 | 25 | 10 | 15 |
| Randall White | 50 | 0 | 30 | 20 |

had sales disproportionately weighted to the feed and farm implement stores in its region. The brand also had strong grocery sales in the Southeast but had yet to crack the national pet food distribution market. All of Randall White's pet food sales were to local mom and pop retailers and dog kennels.

Dry dog food is categorized into two overall product groups, ration—or meal type—brands such as Randall White, and expanded products such as Checkerboard Chow, Gravy Boat, and Puppy Puff, all made by the national marketer, Ralston Dog Food.

Ration-type brands are blended of separate ingredients mixed together in particle form, providing higher protein energy levels in highly concentrated form. They are generally priced at lower levels than expanded products and are most indigenous to the Southeast and Midwest where outdoors activities, including hunting, are the strongest

Expanded products are homogeneous in appearance with all ingredients ground and blended together. They are often "puffed" with air to have a larger than life appearance. Usually they are in "nugget" or simulated "hamburger" form and priced at premium levels. Expanded products are the mainstay of house pets and smaller dogs. Most nationally advertised brands are of the expanded product variety.

In the Southeast, the ration-type brands account for about 40 percent of the market yet nationally, they account for only about 20 percent of the market. Even within the Southeast, the ration-type brand varies markedly by state.

## THE CONSUMER PROFILE

There are three basic markets for dry dog food. The first and largest is the pet dog owner. The second is the hunting/working dog owner. The third is the show dog or

Exhibit 11.3

**Ration-Type vs. Expanded Formula Sales: Geographic Analysis** (in %)

| Geography | % Ration-Type | % Expanded |
|---|---|---|
| National | 20 | 80 |
| Southeast | 40 | 60 |
| Tennessee | 40 | 60 |
| Mississippi/Alabama | 45 | 55 |
| Georgia | 50 | 50 |
| Florida | 25 | 75 |
| Virginia/North Carolina | 20 | 80 |
| South Carolina | 30 | 70 |

pure breed market. This last is a very specialized market with specific niche dog food products tailored to each breed.

Of the two larger markets, each has a distinctive consumer profile. Nationally syndicated research shows the consumer profile for the pet dog owner dog food market to be as follows:

- Women, age 25–49
- Married with children age 5–17
- Attended or graduated college
- Living in suburban areas of highly populated DMAs (designated marketing areas)
- Household income levels of $75,000+
- Owns a single dog

This is contrasted to the consumer market for the hunting/working dog market, which breaks down as follows:

- Men, age 35–64
- Married with either teenage children or no children
- High school education
- Living in C and D counties
- Household income level of less than $75,000
- Owns multiple dogs

On a per capita basis, the hunting/working dog owner is the heaviest consumer of dog food due to its multiple dog ownership. Because he is an extremely heavy user of dog food, the hunting/working dog owner is extremely price conscious.

## RANDALL WHITE CHALLENGE

Within Randall White's marketing area, Randall White has been the number one brand for many years. However, its market share has been consistently eroding over time.

Exhibit 11.4

**Dry Dog Food: Sales by County Size** (in %)

| Southeast County Size | % Population | % Category Sales | % Randall White Sales |
|---|---|---|---|
| A | 22 | 18 | 11 |
| B | 36 | 45 | 31 |
| C | 23 | 21 | 28 |
| D | 19 | 16 | 29 |
| | 100 | 100 | 100 |

Exhibit 11.5

**Randall White Sales and Distribution by State** (in %)

| State | % Sales | % ACV |
|---|---|---|
| Alabama | 20 | 100 |
| Georgia | 18 | 100 |
| Florida | 6 | 40 |
| South Carolina | 13 | 100 |
| Mississippi | 13 | 100 |
| North Carolina | 8 | 70 |
| Tennessee | 14 | 100 |
| Virginia | 8 | 60 |

*Note*: ACV = All Commodity Volume

Exhibit 11.6

**Randall White 5-Year Market Share Trends** (in %)

| | Year 5 | Year 4 | Year 3 | Year 2 | Current Year |
|---|---|---|---|---|---|
| Randall White | 40 | 38 | 33 | 31 | 29 |
| Ralston Brands | 35 | 34 | 34 | 33 | 31 |
| Private Label/Other | 25 | 28 | 33 | 36 | 40 |

Randall White's losses are primarily traceable to the dynamic growth of private-label brands of dry dog food that is priced 30 percent below Randall White.

Other factors are compounding this problem. The first is the urbanization of the Southeast. Fewer and fewer farms are being worked, and with fewer working dogs. The growth of the Southeast has been in large cities and Randall White has been and continues to be more of a rural brand.

The largest factor is that Ralston has begun a specific campaign in the South to launch its new high protein dry dog food mix targeted at large dogs. It is made with 20 percent more protein than Randall White and is sold at a price point 10 percent less than the Randall White brand.

The other day, Randall White sat in this office, thinking about his father's legacy and what he might do in this situation. With his father's death three years ago, Randall

Exhibit 11.7

**Advertising Media Competitive Spending** (000)

| Brand | Spending ($000) | Media Mix |
|---|---|---|
| Ralston Checkerboard Chow | 15,000 | 80% Network TV, 20% Magazine |
| Gravy Boat | 12,500 | 60% Network TV, 40% Magazine |
| Puppy Ruff | 3,000 | 100% Magazine |
| Kennel Club | 6,500 | 100% Spot TV (Pacific, Northeast) |
| Randall White | 1,500 | 100% Spot TV (Southeast) |
| Others | 7,500 | Various |
| Total | 46,000 | |

had assumed the head of the company. He knew that he had to not only arrest the declining share of his market but that he needed to find ways to increase his brand volume.

His marketing people had been hounding him to spend more money on advertising but he had felt that he couldn't compete with Ralston in that arena. His product people had begged him to expand his line into the pet owners' market. His salespeople had felt that, if he expanded his geographical distribution to other feed stores and even other grocery chains, he might not be so vulnerable. His neighbor had said that he had just switched to a private label brand since it was so much cheaper. That really got to Randall. He began to wonder if his product was out of touch with the market.

He knew that he must take some action. So, he asked all of his key management to develop a plan of attack. The question was: What course of action should he take?

## QUESTIONS

1. What analysis do you think that Randall White should ask for to determine his proper course of action?
2. How would you construct a SWOT analysis based on the 4Ps (product, price, place, and promotion) of marketing?
3. Is there any missing information that you would need to make a decision?
4. What decision could you make to have an immediate impact on sales?
5. If Randall White introduced a new product, what would you recommend?
6. What role should advertising play in Randall White's future plans?

# Part V

# Advertising Budget Management

**Case 12 Bosco Hot Sauce Company**
Issue: *Budget Allocation Analysis*

**Case 13 Alpha Airlines**
Issue: *Budget Allocation Analysis*

**Case 14 Southern Rice**
Issue: *Advertising Spending*

Budgeting is perhaps the most important task that an advertising manager must accomplish. For without a proper budget, there is likely to be an ineffective advertising plan.

Even though budgeting for advertising is a crucial exercise, for some it can be daunting, and for those higher up in the organization it can be very frustrating. Advertising budgeting begins with an economics issue and ends in an activity or allocation issue.

From an economics perspective, an advertising manager must be prepared to answer the following questions:

1. What is the relationship between advertising and sales?
2. What is the effective threshold for advertising?
   a. How high is up? Where is the point of diminishing returns?
   b. When is the level too low to have an effect?
3. What is the impact of advertising on each aspect of the brand's purchase funnel, which leads to a consumer buy?
   a. How does advertising impact awareness?
   b. How does advertising impact brand consideration?
   c. How does advertising impact purchase?
   d. How does advertising impact loyalty?

These are not easy questions to answer. Most marketers and advertisers struggle to answer any of them. Yet, they are central to the task of advertising. The only reason to believe in advertising is that it has some sort of impact on the consumer's awareness, intent to purchase, and loyalty toward a brand.

Depending upon statistical sophistication, information available, and the stage in a product's lifecycle, there are a variety of methods used for determining an advertising budget. Some of the more common methods are:

- *Historical Plus Inflation.* Last year the brand spent $1.0 million. We estimate that inflation will be at 5 percent, so this year we will budget at $1.05 million. The advertising spending level is adjusted for inflation so that the brand doesn't lose buying power.
- *Percentage of Sales.* Our brand budgets at 3 percent of sales. So, with $500 million in sales, the advertising budget is $15 million. Many companies and brands use some form of advertising-to-sales ratios to guide their advertising spending.
- *Objective/Task.* Our goal is to achieve a 10 percent market share in the second year so we will spend at 20 percent share of spending to achieve it. Some brands use an analysis that is formed around achieving an objective. There is a body of research that indicates a correlation between advertising investment and market share. To achieve a higher market share, the brand must spend at a disproportionately higher rate than its current market share.
- *Margin Utility.* Our analysis shows that for every dollar spent on advertising we return an incremental $1.50 in sales up to a point of $15 million, where it levels off. Many sophisticated marketing organizations utilize multi-regression analysis to help them budget for advertising based on historical evidence of marginal utility.

Once you have an advertising budget, the next task is to determine how best to allocate the dollars. The allocation of advertising dollars has two key phases:

1. Allocation among different activities.
2. Allocation among various segments within each activity.

The allocation among different activities means how advertising dollars are divided between production of advertising and the placement of advertising. Activities can also mean dividing the budget among sponsorships, media, production, trade shows or events, Web site, and other advertising items.

Within each activity, there are a myriad of segments that can be applied. For example, there are a variety of media that can be chosen for a media plan. Advertising dollars can be allocated differently by geography. Advertising can be allocated differently by timing or seasons. Advertising can be allocated differently based on target market segmentation. Advertising can also be pegged to a certain competitive situation.

Advertising budget allocation can take on many scenarios. How an advertising manager allocates dollars greatly determines the success or failure of the advertising campaign.

In summary, budgeting is an essential advertising management task. To develop an advertising budget requires the advertising manager to consider the economic foundation that underlies the entire advertising and marketing process. There are a wide variety of methods to determine a budget, from historical to sophisticated statistical models. Once an advertising budget is established, the advertising manager must determine how best to allocate those resources. There are a variety of factors in, and uses for, an advertising budget. Allocation of the advertising budget takes into account advertising activities and combines those with various ways of segmenting the budget.

For more information on advertising budget management, see Chapter 10 in Jugenheimer and Kelley's *Advertising Management* textbook.

# Case 12 Bosco Hot Sauce Company

## ISSUE: *Budget Allocation Analysis*

The United States hot sauce market comprises a wide variety of regional and national brands. The total hot sauce market is pegged at $700 million. It is growing at a rate of 7 percent per year.

Regional consumption of hot sauce varies dramatically from the national average. Since hot sauce is colored by regional tastes, the variations of the category can be very extreme.

The Bosco Hot Sauce Company management believes that these regional differences in hot sauce category consumption could be utilized in allocating their advertising dollars. This would be particularly true if the company were to promote the Bosco brand in line with market opportunities and total category potential.

Statistics are given in Exhibit 12.1 for three important markets in which the Bosco Hot Sauce Company is interested in gaining market share. The company plans on investing $1 million in advertising in these three markets next year.

The former marketing manager of Bosco Hot Sauce had been given the assignment of maximizing the effectiveness of the advertising budget. He had begun to work on the task but before he was finished, he abruptly left the company. Now the marketing group is well behind in their planning for the year.

You have just been brought in to manage this brand. One of your first tasks is to finish the analysis that your predecessor had left. How do you tackle it?

## QUESTIONS

1. How would you prioritize the markets based on the analysis?
2. Is there another way that you might analyze the markets to make an allocation decision?
3. Is there information missing from the analysis that would make it better? If so, what is it?
4. What questions doesn't the analysis answer?

Exhibit 12.1

**Bosco Hot Sauce**

| Market | # of HH | % U.S. | Hot Sauce CDI | Total Category $ Volume Millions | Volume Dollars per HH | % Category Volume 3 Markets | Advertising Budget Allocation |
|---|---|---|---|---|---|---|---|
| Nashville | 880,700 | .83 | 110 | | | | |
| Birmingham | 750,000 | .72 | 140 | | | | |
| New Orleans | 650,000 | .59 | 210 | | | | |
| 3 Market Total | 228,700 | 2.14 | | | | | $1,000,000 |
| Total U.S. | | 100 | 100 | $700.0 | | N/A | |

*Note:* HH = Households; CDI = Category Development Index.

# Case 13 Alpha Airlines

## Issue: *Budget Allocation Analysis*

Jim Burns was the advertising manager of Alpha Airlines. He stared at the advertising budget sheet prepared by the media department of his advertising agency, KFM. He was perplexed by the initial pass at how to allocate the budget across his top revenue markets.

Alpha Airlines was positioned as a serious business airline. It had flights only to the top markets in the United States. The goal of Alpha Airlines was to dominate these key markets in the country by having the lowest fares, most flights, and best service. The strategy seemed to be working. Alpha Airlines had been growing steadily since its inception. More established airlines had various strengths in these markets but they typically lacked the strength in each of the top markets. This made them vulnerable to Alpha Airlines.

Jim was told by management that he really needed to grow the Atlanta and Chicago markets. In each of these markets, the current hub carrier was facing financial peril that might bankrupt them. As a result, costs had been cut that had impacted the service level of each of these carriers. Research showed that passengers of these airlines were looking for alternatives. Alpha Airlines was positioned to be that alternative.

With this in mind, Jim scanned the advertising budget document prepared by KFM. The questions and concerns that he had were as follows:

- He was concerned that he was spending the most advertising dollars in Los Angeles. In fact, he was spending more there than in New York. He had been told by the KFM media team that Los Angeles was a very expensive media market but he was concerned that he was overspending the market.
- He also questioned the spending in Atlanta. Hartsfield, the Atlanta airport, was one of the busiest in the world. It was already a strong market for Alpha Airlines, but the advertising spending didn't seem to reflect this.
- He also questioned the light spending in Chicago. Again, here was an opportunity market but the advertising spending didn't seem to reflect this. In fact, the spending in Los Angeles was nearly twice that of Chicago, while Chicago was close on the heels of Los Angeles in terms of revenue.

Exhibit 13.1

**Alpha Airlines Advertising Budget**

| Markets | # of TV HH (000) | Alpha Airlines Revenue (000) | Media Cost (Annual) (000) |
|---|---|---|---|
| New York | 7,082.3 | $215,000 | $10,500 |
| Los Angeles | 5,318.0 | $170,000 | $12,300 |
| Chicago | 3,351.3 | $145,000 | $6,500 |
| Boston | 2,353.5 | $76,000 | $4,750 |
| Dallas/Fort Worth | 2,195.5 | $44,000 | $2,600 |
| Washington, D.C. | 2,169.3 | $50,000 | $3,500 |
| Atlanta | 1,971.2 | $62,000 | $3,100 |
| Total | 24,641.1 | $762,000 | $43,250 |

Jim had told KFM to develop media plans that were the same in all markets so that he could see the impact of the spending. But, he had also told the agency to adjust markets based on his recent input regarding Chicago and Atlanta, and to asterisk them if they were adjusted. Since the agency didn't have an asterisk by the markets, he assumed that they were all the same media plan.

Jim had a budget meeting with his management later that week to discuss how to properly allocate the advertising media dollars by market. He knew that if he took this into the meeting, that it would raise more questions than it answered.

He needed to have the agency develop some other budget scenarios. He wondered if he hadn't given them enough information or proper direction.

"I just keeping getting the same numbers back from the agency," said Jim in frustration to his advertising team.

"Don't they get it?" he added. "Or is it something that I am not giving them," he asked.

Jim called the agency media chief, Bob Alliante, to meet with him and sort it out. He needed a cogent presentation for his management without any holes. As he prepared for his meeting with Mr. Alliante, Jim began to make a list of all the information he needed. What would you put on the list?

## QUESTIONS

1. Based on the advertising budget, how would you analyze the relationship between market size, Alpha Airlines revenue, and media cost?
2. What does the current media budget by market tell you about the media cost in the market?
3. Is there an analysis that you can do to quantify the relationship between the media cost and the market size?
4. What marketing information would help to make this media budget analysis better?
5. What advertising or media information would help to make this analysis more meaningful?
6. What competitive information would help put this analysis into better context?
7. What economic or other information would help add dimension to this analysis?

# Case 14 Southern Rice

## Issue: *Advertising Spending*

The Southern Rice Company is one of the country's leading rice brands. The Southern Rice Company's distribution area is generally equivalent to the territory south of the Mason-Dixon Line with some distribution into western states. The Southern Rice brand is the leading seller among premium-priced brands of rice. The brand costs the consumer approximately 10 cents per pound more than the other leading brands in the market and 20 cents per pound more than private label or store brands.

For more than fifty years, the Southern Rice brand has based its entire marketing and advertising strategy on the sale of a quality brand, which management states costs more due to the natural harvesting technique that they use to cull their rice from the fields. The Southern Rice approach has been a hit with consumers, since a large segment of the population in the southern states indicated that they were willing to pay a bit more to get the type of quality that they enjoy in a rice brand commodity. Price increases for rice in recent times have begun to impact Southern Rice's ability to continue to price its brand at a premium. Consumers have been less willing to pay more for rice as overall food prices continue to increase.

The initial distribution for Southern Rice began in Atlanta where the company was able to obtain a good distribution and acceptance within a short period of time. Management believed that this success was largely due to the association that the brand had with white-tablecloth restaurants that served the product. In fact, Southern Rice was seen as a part of the old southern gentile restaurant scene in Atlanta. Southern Rice used its Atlanta strength to expand to other markets in the south.

Southern Rice was natural long grain rice and was slow-cooked. However, the overall market for slow-cooking rice was dwindling as convenience products entered the picture. Southern Rice saw that its next logical next step was to enter the instant rice market.

At the present time, instant rice is available in a wide variety of physical forms and compositions. The most successful instant rice is made by National Rice, which has national distribution and a strong advertising budget. Instant in a Second by Genfoods is also a strong competitor. Tennessee Tom's rice is another regional competitor and a family operated business just like Southern Rice. Tennessee Tom's is owned by a colorful character, Tom Thibidoux, who is featured in their commercials.

Exhibit 14.1

**Southern Rice Marketing Formula**

2 × SOV = 1 × SOM

*Note:* SOV = Share of Voice; SOM = Share of Market. Spend at least 2 times the category advertising spending to achieve one share point by the second year.

Exhibit 14.2

**Rice Consumption Trends** (lbs. per HH per month)

| Year | Regular Rice | Instant Rice |
|---|---|---|
| YTD—Current Year | 2.70 | 2.39 |
| Past Year | 2.75 | 2.34 |
| 2 Years Ago | 2.85 | 2.30 |
| 3 Years Ago | 2.90 | 2.25 |
| 4 Years Ago | 3.00 | 2.20 |

*Note:* Regular Rice equals 80¢ per lb. while Instant Rice equals $1.50 per lb.
Total: 110 million HH

Exhibit 14.3

**Geographic Analysis**

| Area | Natural Rice CDI | Instant Rice CDI |
|---|---|---|
| New England | 40 | 50 |
| Metro New York | 75 | 95 |
| Middle Atlantic | 110 | 120 |
| East Central | 65 | 70 |
| West Central | 90 | 85 |
| Southeast | 185 | 120 |
| Southwest | 125 | 135 |
| Pacific | 115 | 140 |

*Note*: CDI = Category Development Index.

Instant rice household consumption varies from region to region. A recent article stated that instant rice represented 46 percent of K-Store overall rice sales, in contrast to its overall 30 percent share of the rice category. Another trade release stated that nearly 40 percent of rice sales in the Publix's grocery chain was now instant rice. This was a big trend for Southern Rice since Publix's was the leading grocery chain in the South. K-Store was also important since it was the leading national grocery chain.

Although there are some areas that are strong natural rice areas and weak instant rice areas, the South is strong in all forms of rice consumption. This was a concern for Southern Rice since they did not want to introduce an instant rice that might hurt their own natural rice brand.

Exhibit 14.4

**Instant Rice Goal**

| Year | % Instant Rice Share |
|---|---|
| First Year | 5 |
| Second Year | 10 |
| Third Year | 13 |

Exhibit 14.5

**National Market Share** (in %)

| Brand | Regular Rice | Instant Rice |
|---|---|---|
| Southern Rice* | 20 | — |
| National Rice | 30 | 25 |
| Instant in a Second | — | 30 |
| Tennessee Tom's* | 5 | 5 |
| Private Label | 45 | 40 |

*Southern Rice has 35 percent share in the Southeast while Tennessee Tom's has a 15 percent share in the Southeast.

There were significant differences in who purchased natural rice and instant rice. Natural rice was purchased by large families and it had a distinctive ethnic bias. On the other hand, instant rice attracted singles and small families, and had a more upscale consumer base than natural rice.

The bulk of instant rice advertising funds for the leading brands was used for television. The two national brands, National Rice and Instant in a Second, used national television and some magazines. Tennessee Tom's used only spot television in the key southern markets. However, both the national brands also used spot television in the South to add incremental advertising support in this key region.

The Southern Rice Company is planning on entering the instant rice market in a big way. The markets that they plan on expanding into include Tampa/St. Petersburg, Charlotte, and Washington, D.C. The plan is to obtain a 10 percent market share in sales in these markets within the next two years.

To realize these objectives, Southern Rice management recognizes that it is necessary to spend a substantial amount of advertising. But, they are unclear on how to determine what the appropriate spending level should be.

As a guide to its first efforts in these markets, the company plans a test market program. Results from this test are expected to be in by the end of next year. Southern Rice management expects to launch their marketing program right after the test market results.

The key question for Southern Rice management continued to be the level of spending required to make their market share goals. They turned to their advertising firm, Barkley and Peachtree, to help them determine the number of markets and the level of spending that would be required.

Exhibit 14.6

**Advertising Media Expenditures** (past year current dollars, in millions)

| Brand | Magazine | Net TV | Net Cable | Spot TV | FSI | Total |
|---|---|---|---|---|---|---|
| Southern Rice | 1.0 | — | — | 3.0 | 1.0 | 5.0 |
| National Rice | 2.0 | 8.0 | 2.0 | 3.0 | 5.0 | 20.0 |
| Instant in a Second | 3.0 | 1.0 | 3.0 | 1.0 | 3.0 | 11.0 |
| Tennessee Tom's | — | — | — | 3.5 | — | 3.5 |

Your challenge at the Barkley and Peachtree advertising agency is to determine the advertising spending for each of the two-year periods in the plan and to justify that spending level.

## QUESTIONS

1. How would you approach determining the advertising spending levels?
2. What types of analysis would be the best methods for determining advertising spending levels?
3. Should you consider developing a test market approach? If so, how would you construct a test market scenario?
4. What methods would you consider to justify the spending?
5. What primary research would you consider to aid in determining the advertising spending or the outcome of the advertising?

# PART VI

# ADVERTISING MANAGEMENT: DEALING WITH PEOPLE

**CASE 15 IPORTAL MEDIA COMPANY**
ISSUE: *Employee/Supervisor Review*

**CASE 16 METROPOLITAN MEDIA COMPANY**
ISSUE: *Managing Upward*

**CASE 17 THE DAVIS GROUP**
ISSUE: *Hiring*

**CASE 18 JPT AGENCY**
ISSUE: *Personnel Conflict*

Advertising is a business that deals with people. In fact, managers spend more than two-thirds of their working time dealing with people and people issues.

There is an old saying from a Madison Avenue CEO that goes: "unlike most businesses, all of my assets go up and down the elevator every day." Talented people are the lifeblood of advertising. People also account for the majority of costs for an advertising agency. Typically, 50 percent to 60 percent of the total advertising agency revenue is spent on employee salaries.

How to deal with people and get the most out of them becomes a central role for any manager within the advertising business. One of the key areas that requires effective management is conflict resolution. The advertising business is often rife with conflict. Unlike nearly any other industry, advertising departments or advertising agencies have a wide variety of people and personalities. You have artists, writers, producers, planners, negotiators, business strategists, and financial and administrative personnel. Advertising reflects skill sets ranging from very visual and creative to very business oriented. So, natural conflicts will arise. Advertising is also about taking risks. So, there is a built-in set of conflicts over how much risk a client may take and how strong an advertising agency may push a client to take a risk.

Obviously with such a diverse group of people and range of ages, mind-sets, and culture, there are bound to be daily conflicts that require management attention.

It is then crucial that a manager have strong written and oral communication skills, not only to deal with conflict but to set the tone and effectively communicate with a wide variety of people and personalities. Seventy percent of an adult's waking hours are spent communicating. So, the basics of reading, speaking, and writing are paramount for a manager. However, the corresponding key skill for any manager is to be able to effectively listen. An executive spends more than two-thirds of his or her time just listening. Effective listening is a skill that sets one manager apart from another.

Applying these skill sets to daily advertising management requires patience and maturity. A manager has power, and how he or she chooses to use that power is critical to the business. A manager is involved in hiring, supervising, evaluating, promoting, and paying—all essential personnel functions.

The manager must ensure that all employees understand what they should be doing and how they will be evaluated. Evaluations can be an uncomfortable time for employees, so it is paramount that a manager emphasizes how an evaluation can help develop an employee's career, rather than making it about rewards and punishments.

Managers must provide direction, encourage, motivate, and monitor the work of those who report to them, much as a coach does. Coaching has been a metaphor for management. Managers who are successful as coaches must believe in their people and recognize that employees want to contribute, to work, to learn, to be recognized, and to succeed.

There are many theories about personnel management and management in general. However, there is no single theory about how to manage an advertising agency or an advertising department. Since advertising is an interdisciplinary endeavor, managers in the advertising field can pick and choose the management techniques that fit their style or organization.

One classic management theory is MBO or Management by Objectives. This method is based on setting realistic goals and then establishing action plans to meet them. It is a systematic approach to management and can be effective for setting expectations for an employee. Another classic management theory is TQM or Total Quality Management. TQM is usually associated with manufacturing or production. However, it can be applied to any kind of process. Since advertising has processes to start and complete work, TQM can help make these processes more productive.

These are two of many useful models in management. There are many more that an advertising manager can choose from. It is important for an advertising manager to select what is relevant to his or her situation and not just pick the "flavor of the day." As managers read more on the topic of management, they are sure to discover that some of the approaches actually contradict each other. However, good managers should continue to be good students of management, striving to learn more about how they can become strong leaders, more efficient managers, and more successful executives.

For more in-depth information regarding how to deal with people, please consult Chapters 11, 12, and 13 in Jugenheimer and Kelley's *Advertising Management* textbook.

# Case 15 Iportal Media Company

## Issue: *Employee/Supervisor Review*

Today is the day of a personnel review meeting between Melissa Olson and Billy Malan. Melissa is Billy's supervisor. In fact, Melissa had hired Billy in her group at Iportal Media Company two years ago.

In this case, Melissa and Billy are entering the review with totally opposite viewpoints. The following is each of their viewpoints of Billy's performance.

### Melissa Olson's Viewpoint

I consider Billy Malan to be a very competent worker. His work, in general, is better than most of the other workers at his level. I have given him appropriate raises and have done my best to reinforce his good work.

In spite of his good work record, however, Billy has two very undesirable characteristics. I haven't said anything about them because I thought that they might be corrected naturally. I thought that I could just live with them but now they seem to be getting worse. So, today, I plan to talk to Billy about them.

The first thing I'm going to say to Billy is that he is terribly verbose. This affects not only his writing, but also—particularly—his talking. It takes him twice as much time or space to say things as it should. This is really aggravating because it takes up a lot of my time and it's a reflection on me when my superiors see his work. His coworkers have even begun to joke about his verbosity behind his back. It is really getting out of hand and is having an impact on others' perceptions of my management.

The second item that I'm going to discuss is that Billy is very quick, and finishes his work typically before anyone else. This in and of itself isn't bad, but once he finishes a project, he usually starts clowning around with other employees and many times tells "off-color" jokes. I have tolerated his joking behavior because he does very good work but recently I have had some employees come to me about his behavior. One of them asked, "Can't you keep that clown busy?" Again, Billy's image is getting in the way of his work. And it is beginning to hurt my image as well.

## Billy Malan's Viewpoint

I have worked for Melissa Olson for the past two years. I like the work and do my job very well. Melissa seems to appreciate my work because I have gotten good raises the past two years. I usually finish my work before anyone else and I never have to redo any of it.

If there is one pet peeve that I have, it is that people don't know how to communicate. For one thing, people including Melissa, tend to give me insufficient information and details when they speak and write. I pride myself in taking the extra time necessary to say what I mean clearly and precisely. I don't boil it down to a "sound bite" like everyone else. I know that most people don't get it the first time, so I like to reinforce my messages by carefully repeating my explanations. Although Melissa hasn't told me directly, I think that she appreciates and respects the quality of my work.

That being said, I do sense a change in the business climate. Melissa used to be open and relaxed with me. She even liked my jokes. Now I sense some tension with her. She doesn't take as much time with our group as she had before. She tends to avoid us.

One of the things I really like about this job and the company is that the people do like one another. We enjoy socializing as well as working. After all, it sure makes work a lot better when you can relax and be yourself with everyone. I like to joke around with the other guys, and they seem to like my sense of humor. With Melissa tensing up, I have gone out of my way to tell more jokes to loosen everyone up.

I have aspirations to move up in the company and I hope that Melissa can help me. She is well regarded in the company and I think that she can help me grow and develop. I am looking forward to meeting with her today and discussing how I can take the next step.

## The Meeting

Billy came into Melissa's office for the meeting with a real sense of accomplishment. He was ready to take his career to the next level. Melissa greeted Billy with some sense of dread. How did she tell Billy that he had a couple of serious flaws?

## Questions

1. Who do you think has the best viewpoint, Melissa or Billy?
2. Why do you think that they are so far apart on their views?
3. What could each of them do to gain perspective?
4. Who's responsible for making it right?
5. What should they have done before so that they wouldn't be in this situation now?
6. How do you think that the meeting will go?
7. What do you feel will be the outcome of the meeting?

Case 16

# Metropolitan Media Company

## Issue: *Managing Upward*

Liz Melton was so excited when she joined Metropolitan Media corporation right out of college. This was a dream come true for Liz. Liz had graduated with an advertising degree from a large state university. Through her studies, she had become intrigued with the rapidly changing media landscape and wanted to be a part of it.

Metropolitan Media was a New York-based media conglomerate that owned magazines, cable properties, and online properties. It was one of the first media companies to recognize that there was a digital revolution in the media world. As a result, they were migrating many of their offline media properties to online properties.

Liz was an assistant in the magazine unit working for *New Woman* magazine, one of the largest women's service magazines in the country. Her boss was a 55-year-old woman, Donna Carbone. Ms. Carbone had spent the past 30 years at Metropolitan Media where she rose from a secretarial position to become a senior vice president and publisher of *New Woman.* Ms. Carbone prided herself on the fact that she was the first woman in Metropolitan Media to become an officer of the company. She was a hard-charging and very blunt woman, who got things done but didn't make a lot of friends along the way.

"She is a real old-school woman. Be careful in dealing with her. She is particularly hard on young women starting out. She feels they should be toughened up," said one of Liz's coworkers.

Liz took it all in. She was anxious to set a good career course and get promoted within this exciting company. Her first task was to understand how to best utilize blogs to extend the reach of the magazine into the online world.

Liz threw herself into the project, working 12-hour days for four consecutive weeks. When she wrote a report on her work, Ms. Carbone barely gave her any feedback. Later Liz learned that Ms. Carbone took Liz's report to her management claiming full credit for it.

Ms. Carbone appointed Liz to chair a project committee. This was a great honor. It was very rare that an assistant be assigned to chair such a committee. Liz was thrilled. However, after the committee's work was completed, Liz learned that its recommendations and actions were not what Ms. Carbone wanted. Ms. Carbone had failed to tell her or the committee about a management change that would impact the project. As a result, the outcome was not meeting the new objectives. Not only was the project a bust, but Ms. Carbone was heard making caustic remarks about her and the committee.

"Maybe a few failures will take the wind out of her sails," said Ms. Carbone to another publisher.

When Liz started her job, she was promised a six-month review where she would be considered for a step up in her job responsibilities and a raise. She had approached Ms. Carbone about the review for weeks with no response. Now, it was three months past the review period and Liz was getting very frustrated.

Liz liked her coworkers and the work itself but she was continually frustrated by Ms. Carbone. Liz wondered if others in the management knew of her good work since Ms. Carbone constantly took credit for it. Conversely, Liz was concerned that anytime Ms. Carbone didn't give proper direction, she blamed Liz and others in the department. Finally, Liz felt that she was being treated unfairly regarding her raise. She had been working sixty-hour workweeks since she got to Metropolitan Media and was living on slave wages. She was ready for a bit more money so that she could take advantage of the Manhattan nightlife.

Liz felt that she was at a crossroads with Ms. Carbone and Metropolitan Media. She had to take some action but what?

## QUESTIONS

1. Do you feel that Liz should confront her boss, Ms. Carbone?
2. Do you feel that Liz should seek counsel from the human resource group regarding Ms. Carbone?
3. Do you feel that Liz should go around Ms. Carbone and discuss these issues with a high-ranking officer in the company?
4. Should Liz just wait it out and give it three more months until she has been in the position for a year?

Case 17

# The Davis Group

## Issue: *Hiring*

Jim Davis pondered the two résumés that he had before him. This was a crucial hire for his advertising agency, The Davis Group. Two weeks ago, his top account director had left for another job at a competing advertising agency. If that wasn't enough, the largest account that he was working on, Proctor and Bramble, had said that unless Jim filled the job with a very strong candidate, they would put their account up for review.

Jim quickly hired a recruiter to get qualified candidates for the position. P&B was a tough account and required someone with at least ten years of experience. Due to the nature of the account, Jim also needed someone who had a wide range of experience from package goods to retail. While P&B was a large package goods company, they did a lot of retail promotions. The brands that Jim's agency handled also required that the candidate have experience marketing to women as well as to kids.

The biggest challenge filling the account director position was the candidate's character. The Proctor and Bramble Company had a very formal culture that required you to be highly learned as well as very conservative. It was always a challenge for his creative people to deal with the brand managers of P&B. Jim's creative folks were very liberal and quite artistic, which flew directly in the face of the account's culture. His prior account director was very good at bridging the cultural gap between P&B and the creative group. He needed this candidate to have the same capabilities.

Jim needed to act quickly since P&B would not let much time pass before they made a decision to review their account. Jim couldn't risk that happening. He hoped that either Richard Putnam or Samuel Anderson Cartwright had what it took to replace his account director. Plus he hoped that they would not only fit with P&B but that they would fit his laid-back culture as well.

He had interviewed both of the men on the phone and Richard was by far the best interview. He was glib and had a great sense of humor. Samuel on the other hand was much plainer spoken but seemed like a nice guy.

Jim didn't have a lot of time to make the decision so based on his phone interview and the résumés at hand, he was ready to make the call. Which candidate do you think he should pick?

Exhibit 17.1

**Résumé: Richard Putnam**

**OVERVIEW**
Eighteen years of excellent experience as an account executive, account supervisor, and account coordinator with several outstanding advertising agencies. Record of excellence and achievement in advertising, public relations, and general business communication.

**WORK EXPERIENCE**
- **Platen, Randell, and Plodkin advertising agency, New Rochelle, New York**
Supervisor for all aspects of advertising campaigns, with primary responsibility for success of the programs. Responsible for account supervision on numerous accounts in consumer packaged goods and consumer services. Handled plans for several outstanding advertising and promotional campaigns. Produced first annotated campaign planbook for the agency. Received accolades from many clients for superior quality of work.

- **Creative Advertising Consultants, Inc., Binghamton, New York**
Directed a staff of more than a dozen people, including copywriters, artists, media planners, merchandisers. Participated in all client meetings and planning sessions. Helped establish experimental marketing effort for new product. Oversaw promotional effort for extraordinary new automotive service firm. Selected personnel incentive programs. Organized original seasonal sales program.

- **Rivers, Simon, and Larson advertising, Milwaukee, Wisconsin**
Planned and administered entire advertising program for many clients' accounts. Worked with outstanding regional marketers and advertisers. Created brochures and sales bulletins. Handled all trade show arrangements and business meeting plans. Assisted top management with plans, strategies, and tactics. Credited with "Best of Show" award.

- **Hammacher, Herpel, Mangell, Dover Associates, Mankato, Minnesota**
Section supervisor and account manager. Responsible for creative and media budget of more than half a million dollars. Handled by important local manufacturer. Acted as liaison for staff coordination group meetings. In charge of records for plans board.

- **Wilson/Locke/Inc., advertising agency, Des Moines, Iowa**
Wrote promotional releases. Worked closely with creative staff. Involved in fine client relationship. Honored for outstanding effort.

**EDUCATION**
- Graduate of Coe College, Cedar Rapids, Iowa. Bachelor's degree in liberal arts. 1978.
- Candidate for master's degree in business, University of Wisconsin, Milwaukee. Writing a thesis on "Advertising Management in Computer Age."
- Honors: Iowa State scholarship, $1,500 awarded in competitive exam.
- Dean's List.
- Kappa Mu honorary.

**PROFESSIONAL EDUCATION**
- Attended two-week training seminar, Glendale, California. Worked with distributors and wholesalers in research and development program for new and improved products.
- Graphic training course.
- Management planning seminar, New York City.
- Dale Carnegie Institute.

**PERSONAL INFORMATION**
Born in Waterloo, Iowa. Attended Dubuque, Iowa, public schools.
Divorced; one daughter.
Hobbies: reading, travel, crafts.
Current address: 1414 Northern Avenue, Apt. 34C, New Rochelle, New York 14664. Telephone 914-322-5588

**REFERENCES**
Best personal and business references are available.

Exhibit 17.2

**Résumé: Samuel Anderson Cartwright**

**Business Address:** Gothan, Rainer Marketing Consultants, Inc.
147 Broadway, Suite 3314
New York, New York 10012
Telephone (212) 596-9383, ext. 21

**Home Address:** Apartment 433, Lewis Towers
1414 East 46th Street
New York, New York 10014

**Career Objective:** Advertising managerial position, either as an advertising agency account executive, or as a brand manager in the marketing or advertising department of a major corporation.

**Experience:**

- Marketing consultant with Gothan, Rainer Marketing Consultants, New York City, March 2005–present.
  Involved in the planning and execution of advertising and marketing pro grams for Ideal Toy Company, Burlington Industries, and SCM Corporation.

- Advertising manager, Butler Brothers discount store chain, Trenton, New Jersey, February 2001–March 2005.
  Responsible for budgeting, media selection, special promotion planning, and marketing coordination for seventeen large discount stores in Pennsylvania, New York, Maryland, Delaware, and New Jersey.

- Account coordinator, Blandell & Rupee advertising agency, Pittsburgh, Pennsylvania, September 1990–February 2001.
  Supervised accounts for small local retail store, for regional dog food manufacturer, for fast-food chain operation and for agricultural custom fertilizing service.

- Account trainee and copywriter, Blandell & Rupee advertising agency, Pittsburgh, Pennsylvania, July 1989–September 1989.
  Wrote copy and created promotional campaigns and advertisements for various accounts, including a ski shop, a small automotive parts supplier, and an industrial packaging distributor.

**Education:** B.S. degree in business, Indiana State University, Indiana, Pennsylvania, June 1989.

**Personal:** Born December 7, 1968, in Cleveland, Ohio. Reared in Akron, Ohio, and Youngstown, Ohio. Attended public schools. Married: two children, wife employed in own public relations firm in New York City. Hobbies include boating, golf, tennis, bridge, antique collecting and refinishing. Member of New York Advertising Club; regional vice president of United Way campaign, 1996–present.

**References:**

- Mr. William Rainer; executive vice president; Gothan, Rainer Marketing Consultants (address above).
- Mr. Henderson Butler; Butler Brothers Stores, Inc., P.O. Box 14, Trenton, New Jersey 08354.
- Additional references available on request.

## QUESTIONS

1. Do you think that Jim Davis has enough information to make a decision?
2. Based on the resumes, which candidate appears the best qualified for the position?
3. What are the differences between the two candidates?
4. Is there anything about Richard Putnam's resume that would raise any red flags in terms of hiring?
5. Is there anything about Samuel Anderson Cartwright's background that would raise any red flags in terms of hiring?

Case 18

# JPT Agency

## Issue: *Personnel Conflict*

You knew that the general manager's job in the Houston office of JPT was dangerous when you took it. Phil Silverman was the creative director of the office. While he was one of the most creative guys on the planet, he was also one of the most volatile.

For every great idea he had, he had many more that ignored the basic marketing strategies established by the client. It seemed that the more off strategy he was, the more stubborn he became about his ideas.

Yesterday, he clashed directly with the president and marketing director of one of your most important clients. Today you've called him into your office to discuss it. You explain to him that you were embarrassed about his performance, particularly in light of the fact that the creative was completely off strategy.

Phil said that he didn't appreciate you taking the client's side in front of the entire agency account group and creative team. Phil went on to say, "If you're going to undercut me like that then my value is nil."

Phil went on to say that he thought that the client had the wrong strategy and that his creative would be on strategy if they would listen to his reasoning.

"The next time we present creative, I don't want any one else in the room with the client but me," said Phil dramatically.

He stormed out of your office saying, "If you don't let me present the creative that I want, then I'm through here."

How do you handle this situation?

## Question

1. Should you have seen the creative prior to having it being shown to the client?
2. Should you have Phil resign?
3. Should you discuss Phil's importance to the account with the client before you make a decision?
4. Should you discuss Phil's performance with others in the office?
5. If Phil leaves, how should you handle it with the rest of the staff or the clients?

# Part VII

# Advertising Management Decisions

**Case 19** **Barrands Agency**
Issue: *Advertising Spokesperson*

**Case 20** **Zeller Group**
Issue: *Client Trade-off*

**Case 21** **Boston Life Insurance**
Issue: *Advertising Strategy*

Advertising managers make decisions all the time. Some decisions can be reached after a period of study—say, in long-range planning; others have to be made on the spot. However, whatever the decision, some form of strategic thinking is involved.

In strategic thinking, one must consider both the implementation of the decision as well as of its impact on future plans. In other words, you must make a decision that can be implemented and that lies within the overall framework of what you are trying to do in the long run. This sounds rather simple, but obstacles along the way can make it more difficult.

Sometimes decisions can be based on statistical data. But, more often than not, managers are asked to make decisions with incomplete data. Since advertising is very fast paced, decisions must be made quickly, and that may mean little or no data are available at the time.

Advertising management decisions can be made by an individual, but many times they are made in a group setting. Group dynamics tend to make decisions that are more conservative than those made by a single decision maker. However, group dynamics can be influenced by a dominant personality, which may derail the best decision for one that best fits that person's agenda.

There are four types of advertising decisions: optimal (the best decision), beneficial (better than harm), neutral (no benefit and no harm, or equal benefits/equal harm), and harmful (more harm than good).

Although it may seem intuitive to try to make the optimal decision, doing so often requires lots of time and information. Most marketing and media decisions are made at only a .4 level of confidence. That means, for every decision you make, there is about a 60 percent probability of its not being optimal and only a 40 percent confidence that you are correct. So, how does business operate in such a vague world?

One way of dealing with decisions is to set up a decision tree. Decision trees can become complex algorithms. However, they can be as simple as answering the following questions:

1. What are the options? (Actions might we take)
2. What are the relevant uncertainties? (Events that might occur)
3. What are the possible outcomes? (Consequences or actions)
4. What is important to the decision maker? (Criteria for the manager)

This type of input can form a statistical input if you apply various weights to the steps and the outcomes. It can become as complex or as simple as you care to make it.

Practical decision making is no more complex than listing the advantages and disadvantages of the decision on a piece of paper and assigning values to each one.

Advertising management decisions are a part of life. Involving a group in the decision-making process has both pros and cons. There are a variety of decision techniques, such as decision trees and statistical decision analysis that can help make sound decisions. All decisions must serve two masters. They must be practical enough to be implemented and solid enough to fit within the overall framework of the long-term strategic plan.

For more information on advertising management decisions, consult Chapters 14 and 15 of Jugenheimer and Kelley's *Advertising Management* textbook.

Case 19

# Barrands Agency

## Issue: *Advertising Spokesperson*

Lisa Blunt, account director of the Barrands Agency, couldn't believe her eyes when she surfed the Internet for the news headlines this morning. She quickly turned on the television to see if she could confirm it. Yes, it was true.

Britney Spice had been caught with a bag of marijuana in her car after she was stopped for erratic driving at 3 o'clock that morning in Los Angeles. This wasn't the first time that Britney had been in trouble with the law. She was a known kleptomaniac and had taken a wig and four coats last month from a dress shop in Beverly Hills. She even was caught shoplifting a cigarette lighter from a convenience store just two weeks ago. But, she had never been caught with drugs.

Britney Spice was the spokesperson for one of the Barrands Agency clients, Glam Girl, a new beauty product line-up, that was taking the teenage market by storm. Britney Spice was the perfect spokesperson since she had a number one hit single record and was in a variety of television sitcoms watched by teenage girls. Britney had cultivated that "clean-cut teen idol" image that fit with what Glam Girl was all about.

Tim Barrands, founder and president of the Barrands Agency, came into Lisa's office and said, "Lisa, we need to call our lawyers and begin to cancel Britney's contract with Glam Girl and alert the media team to immediately cancel our ads. We need to be proactive on this issue before the client calls."

Just after Tim left her office, Bobbi Hazeltine, the creative director, came into Lisa's office and said, "Thank God that girl got caught with some pot. I hated working with her and her agent. Frankly, I am the one that needed drugs to tolerate her."

After hearing Tim and Bobbi, Lisa was figuring out how to break this to the client when Judi Mitchell, the head of the company's public relations division, strode into Lisa's office and said, "Lisa, this is the break we were looking for. Glam Girls needs to be a bit more 'bad girl' and this is our break. And if we stay with Britney while she is down, we can be there as she rises out of rehab. You know, they say that any publicity is good publicity. Well, we can get millions of dollars of publicity for Glam Girls out this."

Now Lisa's head was reeling. She needed a clear strategy to deal with this situation and call the client with a point of view, but it wasn't clear what she should do.

"Lisa, Jim Walters of Glam Girl is on the phone and wants to talk to you as soon as possible," said Lisa's assistant Beverly.

Beverly added, "Jim really sounds mad. You better call him now."

Lisa picked up the phone and began to dial Jim's number. "I hope that what I say is right," she thought.

## QUESTIONS

1. What should Lisa counsel her client to do?
2. What is the most ethical course of action?
3. Is the ethical course of action the best business strategy?
4. Is this an advertising issue or a legal issue or both?
5. How would you change a spokesperson without damaging the brand?

Case 20

# Zeller Group

## Issue: *Client Trade-off*

Betsy Zeller, president of Zeller Group, sat in her office pondering the call she had just received from an agency search consultant. The consultant had said that the client she represented, Universal Healthcare Systems, was very interested in having her agency pitch their business. The client was familiar with the agency's work and thought that they would be a good fit. However, there was one catch. Intrepid Healthcare, a small hospital chain that Betsy had handled for twenty years, would be a conflict. If they proceeded with the review for Universal Healthcare Systems, they would have to resign Intrepid Healthcare.

Intrepid Healthcare was the second account the Zeller Group had landed. In fact, Betsy had handled the account personally for the initial eight years that Intrepid was at the agency. Intrepid was never very large, but they did do nice work. The past two years, Zeller Group was awarded a Health Effie, one of the highest awards for healthcare advertising. However, Intrepid was now one of the smallest accounts at the agency and was never going to be big.

Universal Healthcare Systems, on the other hand, was one of the top three healthcare systems in the country. They were in thirty states and had a huge advertising budget. Their entire account would represent nearly 50 percent of the Zeller Group's total revenue. They were a big-time client and would represent a big step forward for the Zeller Group if the agency was fortunate enough to win the account. However, Universal Healthcare Systems was not without its own baggage. They had a track record of changing agencies every three years. They had also had a series of accounting scandals that had greatly impacted their stock price. It was not known if their current CEO would survive this scandal or if the board of directors would replace him with a new CEO. While the agency search consultant told Betsy that all of this would have no impact on the Chief Marketing Officer and the advertising budget, Betsy had to wonder if this was really true.

Betsy took out a pencil and on a big pad began to write the possible decisions that she would have to make.

1. Pass on Universal Healthcare Systems and retain Intrepid. In fact, she could use this to further cement the Intrepid relationship.
2. Resign Intrepid and pitch Universal in hopes of winning the account. Of course, if she lost, then the agency would have lost both accounts.
3. Discuss the situation with Intrepid and ask permission to pitch the Universal account and not resign Intrepid unless they won the account.
4. Don't discuss this with Intrepid and pitch the account and then make the decision once she learned if she won or lost.

All of these decisions had possible pros and cons. Pitching Universal Healthcare Systems was a high-risk but high-reward situation. There weren't many accounts this size that the Zeller Group had pitched. Betsy knew that most agencies would jump at the chance to pitch such a large piece of business. However, Betsy prided herself on her integrity as well as her business acumen. She thought, "This decision is really a test of both of these. I hope that I make the right decision."

## QUESTIONS

1. What decision do you think that Betsy Zeller should make?
2. Are there any other decision alternatives that she should consider?
3. Is there other information that she needs to make this decision?
4. Should she consult with other members of the agency before making this decision?
5. Is this totally a business decision or are there any ethical issues to consider?

# Case 21 Boston Life Insurance

## Issue: *Advertising Strategy*

Boston Life Insurance was founded in 1890 as one of the first life insurance companies in the United States. As with most insurance companies, Boston Life had diversified into a financial services company through a variety of acquisitions. Boston Life had an extensive marketing sales force throughout the United States.

Boston Life was the third largest life insurance company, offering traditional life insurance policies as well as annuity products and other financial instruments. The top insurance company was Peoples Insurance followed closely by Mutual Insurance. Metro Insurance was the fourth largest insurance company in the category but they were far down the line from the top three in terms of market share.

## Boston Life Advertising Strategy

Boston Life management believed that the company had evolved over the years from one that provided only life insurance to one that provided for the entire family's financial foundation. According to a recent study, Boston Life customers found the brand to be:

- Responsive to their needs.
- Good to do business with.
- A moral and ethical company.
- Solid and stable.

However, even though Boston Life had some positive attributes, Carl Morgan, the advertising director of Boston Life, wanted to take it up a notch. His goals for the company and the agency were for Boston Life to be positioned as the leader in the category and to increase its awareness among a younger population of potential families. Carl was concerned that Boston Life was missing out on the younger end of the market by not marketing to them effectively and by not aggressively using the sales force to call on this audience.

Exhibit 21.1

**Top-of-Mind Awareness** (in %)

| Company | Wave 1 | Wave 2 | Wave 3 | Wave 4 |
|---|---|---|---|---|
| Boston | 17 | 21 | 18 | 17 |
| Mutual | 8 | 11 | 13 | 15 |
| Metro | 13 | 12 | 11 | 11 |
| Peoples | 25 | 24 | 25 | 24 |

*Source:* Boston Life Insurance
*Sample:* 1,000 respondents per wave.

Exhibit 21.2

**Top-of-Mind Awareness by Key Demographics**

| | Demographics | Boston Wave 4 (%) |
|---|---|---|
| Gender | Men | 24 |
| | Women | 15 |
| Age | 18–34 | 9 |
| | 35–54 | 19 |
| | 55+ | 26 |
| Education | Less than college | 17 |
| | College + | 19 |
| HH Income | Less than $50K | 15 |
| | $50K to $100K | 18 |
| | $100K+ | 20 |
| | Overall | 17 |

*Source:* Boston Life Insurance
Sample = 1,000

Carl was also not convinced that the current advertising campaign, "Special Moments for Special Families," was hitting the mark. He felt that it was nice but that it wasn't truly a breakthrough campaign or that it really differentiated Boston Life from its competitors.

## ADVERTISING TRACKING RESEARCH

Jim Walters, the account director of Peabody Agency, began to survey the recent results of the advertising research for Boston Life. He had taken many calls from Carl Morgan regarding the Boston Life campaign. Jim knew that Carl wanted more from the campaign.

However, Jim also knew that every time that Peabody Agency had suggested a change in strategy, the CEO of Boston Life had turned it down. He was very conservative and wanted to stay the course with the advertising.

As Jim looked over the advertising research, he saw things that did not make him

Exhibit 21.3

**Boston Creative Testing**

| Diagnostics | Boston Score | Financial Services Norms |
|---|---|---|
| Recall of ad | 20 | 21 |
| Playback of key message | 10 | 15 |
| Likeability of ad | 35 | 22 |
| Positive image | 31 | 28 |
| Unique to advertiser | 15 | 18 |

happy. The first thing that he reviewed was the top-of-mind awareness numbers from a national survey that Boston Life did with over one thousand consumers. The study had surveyed both customers and noncustomers to understand where they stood in the market in terms of overall awareness and advertising awareness compared to the key competitors.

The top-of-mind awareness numbers for Boston Life continued to go down. They had peaked in Wave 2 of the study but now they were actually back to where they had started in Wave 1. What was even more disturbing was that Mutual Life Insurance was beginning to gain momentum. They were closing in on Boston Life. The top brand, Peoples, continued to plug away as number one.

When Jim turned the page of the study to the demographic breakdown of the awareness numbers, his heart dropped further. He started to see where the Boston Life advertising campaign was having an impact and where it was sorely lacking.

It was obvious from this chart that Boston Life was being effective with older, more upscale men. However, they were woefully underdeveloped with the younger end of the family set and with women.

"No wonder Carl Morgan is concerned with our advertising campaign," thought Jim.

## CREATIVE TESTING RESEARCH

Jim Walters wasted no time in calling his team together after the tracking study research was in. He said, "We must determine if our media plan or our message or both are on track." Jim felt that this was a critical time for the agency to do something on the account. So, he commissioned creative testing research that the agency paid for at its own expense.

The creative testing research was done with Boston Life ads put into the advertising medium with other ads. This was done for Boston Life with both television and print advertising. For the television ads, they were placed within the context of a 30-minute television program and in commercial pods with other ads. Consumers were then asked to recall ads in the program and then replayed the Boston Life ad for specific feedback. A similar test was done with newspapers where a consumer was asked to read the newspaper and then asked about the ads within it.

The scores of the consumer responses were then compared against other financial services companies that had also done this type of creative testing. These were called

Exhibit 21.4

**Competitive Media Spending** (millions of dollars)

| Company | Year 1 | Year 2 | Year 3 |
|---|---|---|---|
| Boston | 15.0 | 18.0 | 21.0 |
| Mutual | 6.0 | 8.0 | 9.0 |
| Metro | 8.0 | 8.0 | 7.0 |
| Peoples | 20.0 | 22.0 | 24.0 |

normative values. Jim Walters was anxious to understand if the Boston Life ads were better than the normative values.

What Jim found was a mixed bag. The overall recall of the Boston Life ad was right on norm but consumers didn't play back the key message of the commercial. Consumers really liked the ads yet they didn't feel that they were unique to Boston Life.

Jim wasn't sure what to do with the results. The campaign was a series of warm family moments so he wasn't surprised if consumers liked them. "Who doesn't like cuddly kids and their pets," he thought. What bothered Jim was the diagnostics on uniqueness. That was what Carl Morgan of Boston Life had been harping about. Yet the CEO of Boston Life loved the ads. "I feel so good when I see them," said the CEO.

## MEDIA ANALYSIS

The bigger news in analyzing the advertising strategy for Boston Life was in the competitive media analysis. Boston Life had steadily been increasing its advertising expenditures for the past three years. It was closing in on the category leader, Peoples Insurance.

As Jim reviewed the media expenditure information, he also saw that Mutual Life had increased their spending, yet they were still spending less than half of Boston Life's total.

"We have been spending more, yet we seem to be getting nowhere in terms of top-of-mind awareness," thought Jim. Jim knew that this chart alone was a condemnation of an ineffective advertising program. He mused, "I don't think too many clients are willing to spend more and get the same thing."

As Jim dove deeper into the information, he began to see where differences emerged in the way the media dollars were allocated by each of the brands. His media group had provided a breakdown of the four insurance companies and the major media in which they invested their advertising dollars.

Boston Life had had the same media mix for years. They had been very print-focused. This was due to the Boston Life's CEO, who felt that a product like life insurance should have a medium that is tangible.

"Print conveys that we are a real company. Plus it is great to send those ads to our sales force," commented the Boston Life CEO. The past few years, Boston Life had

Exhibit 21.5

**Media Mix Analysis** (in %)

| Medium | Boston | Mutual | Metro | Peoples |
|---|---|---|---|---|
| Network TV/Cable | 30 | | 10 | 70 |
| National/Spot Radio | | 60 | | |
| Magazine | 30 | | 40 | |
| Newspaper | 30 | | | |
| Out-of-Home | | 30 | | |
| Sponsorships | 10 | | 40 | 20 |
| Online | | 10 | 10 | 10 |
| Total | 100 | 100 | 100 | 100 |

developed a series of television ads that were placed in golf and tennis programming. Boston Life also sponsored a series of yacht races that began in Boston Harbor. The Boston Life CEO was an avid sportsman and he enjoyed being associated with yachting, golf, and tennis.

Jim found it interesting that Peoples Insurance spent the majority of their dollars on network television and cable television. You expected that type of media plan from the category leader. Mutual Insurance took a different tack. They have developed a funny character that had a recognizable voice. As a result, they put their money into radio and did selective markets with outdoor.

## ADVERTISING DECISIONS

Jim felt that he had all the information he needed to help craft a point of view on Boston Life. He wondered how he should put it together and what he should actually reveal to the client. This was going to be a difficult meeting, since much of the advertising strategy had been directed by the Boston Life CEO. Yet, Jim knew that the agency was ultimately responsible for the advertising program.

Jim also knew that Carl Morgan wanted results and would not be satisfied unless something was changed to make the program more effective. Jim saw issues with both the creative and the media—but which one was really driving the lower awareness numbers? Jim wondered if wholesale changes were needed or if he should just redirect some dollars into different media. He was particularly troubled by the program in light of the lack of response of younger families.

Jim had a week to prepare for a meeting where he would address both Carl Morgan and the Boston Life CEO with some answers. He started to work that afternoon on the agency point of view.

## QUESTIONS

1. What do you think the agency point of view should be regarding the Boston Life advertising?
2. What changes would you recommend to reach younger families?

3. Do you think that the media plan should be significantly changed? If so, what changes would you make?
4. Do you think that the creative should be changed?
5. How do you think Jim Walters should handle the issue of creative testing with the client? What should he tell him, if anything?
6. What should Carl Morgan, as a client, demand from the agency?
7. Knowing the Boston Life CEO's involvement, how much should Carl Morgan hold the agency responsible for the advertising results?

# PART VIII

# ADVERTISING MANAGEMENT ENVIRONMENT

**CASE 22 ZOOMRA MOTORCYCLES**
**ISSUE:** *Media Vendor Conflict*

**CASE 23 GLIB MEDIA**
**ISSUE:** *Sales Incentives Ethics*

**CASE 24 TEXSIZE OIL**
**ISSUE:** *SEC Code Violation*

Advertising management decisions are made within a larger context. That environmental context refers to both outside and personal influences. Outside influences are public policy that forms the foundation for our legal principles and regulations. Personal influences include the ethics of both yourself and your organization.

To be an effective manager, you must be aware of public policy. You must know which way the government is leaning when it comes to regulation, and also have a thorough understanding of the actual laws, rules, and regulations that are established by the federal, state, or local communities where you may work.

Advertising is impacted by a variety of regulators on a federal, state, and sometimes local level. The federal government regulates advertising through the media. The Federal Communications Commission, or FCC, is the federal legislative body that oversees media and helps govern what can be said in the media.

National media will demand that an advertiser have substantiation for any product claims that may be made in advertising. These claims may need substantiation from other federal governing agencies, such as the Federal Drug Administration for pharmaceutical advertising. Understanding what claims can be made and what is deemed appropriate or not appropriate to communicate is a crucial part of any advertising manager's role.

There is nothing more frustrating or costly than developing an advertising campaign and not being able to air it due to legal constraints. The majority of advertisers use legal counsel to vet their messages prior to airing them to avoid these types of situations.

Any form of communication is subject to copyright, trademark, and logo protection. Again, gaining copyright or trademark protection is an important part of any advertising campaign, since intellectual property should be protected as a competitive advantage.

Advertising managers must deal with legal issues. But, they must also deal with moral issues as well. There is always the joke that advertising ethics is an oxymoron. However, personal and organizational ethics in advertising are central to the survival of your career and the reputation of your company.

As a manager, you will be faced with personnel issues that will be ethical problems. For example, do you turn a blind eye when you know someone is taking more than his or her share of supplies? Or do you turn in someone you know is freelancing on the side but using agency resources to do these projects? Or what do you do when a client asks you to hire his son or daughter? All of these examples are ethical situations.

As a manager, you will also be exposed to confidential information. If you work for an advertising agency, you may be asked to sign a nondisclosure agreement, which means that you can be legally liable for telling someone confidential information about that company. You may know if a company is launching a new product, or if it is in trouble long before others know of this. This type of information can be valuable to others. It can be tempting to use this information for personal gain.

You will also be in a position where you select vendors to work with. These can be production companies, media outlets, consultants, and research companies, among others. Depending upon their financial or ethical situation, companies may offer you incentives to do business with them. This raises ethical issues for both you and your organization.

The organization has a number of ethical considerations. It must do what is right for the company, the stockholders, the employees, and the clients and vendors. But, all organizations have a social contract. That is, they have a social responsibility. Good businesses should have a social conscience. They should want to enhance the community they live in and make the industry they operate in a better one.

Due to the public influence that advertising can wield, advertisers, advertising agencies, and media outlets give their time and money to promoting social causes. National advertising campaigns to promote more responsible drinking and driving, and to stop drug use, are all examples of working for the greater good of society.

In summary, advertising managers must understand the public policy environment and operate in a manner that is not only legally correct but morally right. Business ethics rise from personal ethics. Individuals and organizations have a social responsibility. The manager has a crucial role in establishing a firm's ethical and social responsibility standards.

For more information regarding advertising management environment, please consult Chapters 16 and 17 in Jugenheimer and Kelley's *Advertising Management* textbook.

# Case 22 Zoomra Motorcycles

## Issue: *Media Vendor Conflict*

Jim Fuller is a media representative extraordinaire. He is knowledgeable about his product and your client, plus he is persistent without being a pest. To some in your agency, he can be annoying. This is particularly true of the account people and some of the junior media people. However, since you are the media director, you understand that much of Jim's compensation is based on how much he sells.

"You would be aggressive too if your income depended upon how much you sold," you told one of the media supervisors.

In recent weeks, your agency has been finalizing the coming year's advertising program for your key account, Zoomra Motorcycles. Zoomra had been positioned as a motorcycle for weekend enthusiasts but now the company was making a big push into the youth market. This was based on the success of their recent X-Games motocross wins.

This new target is a big departure from the past three years. However, Zoomra's advertising manager, his boss, the vice president of advertising, and the chief marketing officer are all on board with the new strategy. This new strategy has required a new media plan and your Zoomra media team have drafted a plan that consists of some teen publications as well as a strong online presence to support the effort. Some of the prior year's media were retained to maintain some baseline support to the suburban audience but it was reduced by more than 50 percent to fund the new target effort.

One of the changes to the plan involved dropping the publications that Jim Fuller represented in favor of new publications that offered better coverage of the new communications objective. Your media team reviewed the changes to the media schedule but the media team did not go into detail over the elimination of many of the prior year's commitments. But, the client did review the schedule and raised no objections in the meeting. You had also reviewed the plan and approved of the changes but you were aware that Jim Fuller would fight for his publications to be on the schedule. When you asked your media team about any issues with the client, they said that there were none.

In the preceding three years, Fuller's publications had carried an intensive schedule of color spreads for Zoomra. Your spending in his publications totaled nearly $1 million, which likely netted him a commission well into the six figures.

When Fuller learned of the change from your media department, he came in to see you. He argued that the proposed action was a mistake, and that other media should be substituted to fund the new program and not his.

"My publications have been the backbone of this plan for years and now you are cutting them all out. It just doesn't make any sense," Jim Fuller argued.

He went on to say that he didn't believe that Zoomra's advertising manager or CMO had grasped the significance of the changes to the media plan. You listened to him patiently and explained the reasons for the changes based on your media team's thinking.

"Jim, I know that this means a lot of money to you but it is the right thing to do for the brand," you told him.

Jim Fuller stormed out of your office and said that he did not intend to lose this business and that you would hear from him soon.

A week later, Jim Fuller calls you and requests an appointment. When he arrives in your office, he drops a bombshell on you.

"I've just come from a session with Zoomra management where I went over my publications story and how it would be a mistake to kill our program. They agree with me that it would be a colossal mistake to drop us from their media schedule next year. You will be getting a call from them to reinstate us at last year's levels and to rework the media plan to accommodate us."

Jim Fuller added, "I told Zoomra that I wanted to let you know about the decision promptly and they said that I could tell you it was a firm decision. Since we are in, I would be happy to help you rebuild the media schedule so that the total dollars doesn't exceed the budget."

You looked at Jim Fuller with a stunned look on your face. You struggled to determine what you should do. You needed to take some action but what?

## QUESTIONS

1. What should you tell Jim Fuller?
2. What should you have done to prevent this situation from happening in the first place?
3. Should you call in your media team to confront Jim?
4. Should you call the client and confirm Jim's stance?
5. Should you ask the client to reconsider if he has added Jim's publications to the schedule?

Case 23

# Glib Media

## Issue: *Sales Incentives Ethics*

Bob Harrell was the national sales manager of Glib Media. Glib Media was a new medium built around celebrity profiles and interviews. It began as an online chat room and now was a true medium with over one million unique visitors every month. Glib had expanded beyond just online to also offer a monthly magazine. It was now a multi-media company with a national audience that rivaled many well-known media companies.

Bob Harrell started the sales effort by himself in a tiny office in a warehouse in San Francisco. That was where the company was founded. Initially formed with only ten employees, Glib now employed nearly one hundred people who worked on the Web site and the magazine. Bob was challenged to quickly build a national sales team. He had a couple of choices. One was to hire and train a sales force himself. The alternative was to hire established media rep firms to represent his property to advertisers and agencies.

After much debate within the brick walls of Glib Media, Bob persuaded his management to establish a commission deal with existing media rep companies as a means of quickly ramping up a national sales arm. Bob said that this was the quickest way to set things into motion. Existing media rep firms already had the advertising contacts that would take months for Glib Media to establish, and they all had track records that were easy to check. It seemed like the right path for a rapidly growing media company to expand their sales.

After interviewing and hiring media representatives in New York, Chicago, Atlanta, Dallas, and Los Angeles, Bob had a national sales meeting with his new sales force team. He told them that Glib Media was going to offer them a sliding scale commission based on how much they sold. The first million of sales would be at 20 percent commission, the second million would be at 30 percent commission, and anything above three million dollars would be at a 40 percent commission. The only stipulation that Bob gave each of the sales teams was that he would discount his rates by only 20 percent.

"I have found that Glib Media has a good franchise and that we don't need to deeply discount our rates to attract advertisers. I am not going to play the deep discount game. That is why I have developed the rate card to be competitive without deeply discounting our product," said Bob to the sales team.

Bob was satisfied with his decision to build his sales force through the use of media rep firms. He immediately saw the results as his Chicago and Atlanta sales teams each pulled in more than a million dollars worth of media sales within the first two weeks of being assigned the business.

In week three, Bob got a call from the president of the media rep firm in New York, Saul Libowitz. Saul asked Bob for a special discount of 25 percent so that he could close a deal.

Saul said, "Look, everyone in New York discounts media at least 25 percent. I can have a $10 million deal with Mega Media, the largest media buying firm in the world, if you will give a bit on the discount."

Bob said that if he allowed Saul to discount by more than 20 percent, then he would have to let the rest of the sales teams do it as well.

"I have already turned down deals in Dallas and Los Angeles that involved more than 20 percent discounts. How can I let you do it and not let the other guys do it," Bob asked Saul.

"Well, you don't have to offer it to everybody. You can offer it just to us. We will sell more advertising in New York than the rest of the country combined. So, let us do what we need to do," demanded Saul.

Saul added, "While you are at it, we need a higher commission rate than the rest of the firms since we are probably going to be somewhere in the $40 million level of sales. Just let us know what you want to do and let's start making some money."

Bob hung up the phone and sighed. So, this is what his management had warned him about regarding the downside of not building his own sales force. He is too far in now to turn back. He thought, "What should I do?"

## QUESTIONS

1. Should Bob cut a special deal with Saul?
2. Is it ethical to have different deals with the various media rep firms?
3. Should Bob amend his stance on his media discount structure for all the firms?
4. Should Bob ask Saul if he can speak to the Mega Media agency and persuade them to accept a lower discount structure on their media buy?
5. Should Bob look for other media rep firms to represent him in New York and fire Saul?

Case 24

# Texsize Oil

## Issue: *SEC Code Violation*

In your job as chief communications officer for Texsize Oil, you are constantly exposed to highly confidential material. As a corporate officer, you are bound by a fiduciary duty to not disclose any confidential information to anyone or to act on that information to better yourself.

The latest meeting involved a strategy discussion of how to get more deeply involved with the area of green energy. With the national push to reduce America's dependence on oil, plus the burgeoning green movement, Texsize Oil had been on the hunt for companies to acquire to help it diversify its revenue streams.

During that meeting, Jim Hand, the CEO, presented an acquisition opportunity that was mind-boggling. Mr. Hand's acquisition team had found a microbiology company, Green Steam, which had developed a microbe that would turn water into an instant energy form.

"Why, this will not only revolutionize the oil business but it will impact all energy forms as we know them today," said Mr. Hand. Mr. Hand turned to you and said, "Talk about an advertising campaign. This is better than Edison launching the first lightbulb."

Everyone in the room was stunned by the huge effect this would have on the company. This was the type of breakthrough that everyone in the world was looking for. The impact would be staggering—not only on business but on a wide variety of social problems such as third world energy needs.

As you left the meeting, the CFO, Bob Freeman, took you aside and said, "I am going to call my stockbroker and buy as much Teledyne stock along with our own Texsize stock that I can afford." Mr. Freeman went on to say that Teledyne was a company that made water filters. They were the only company that Green Steam could use to get their microbes into the water system. Since Teledyne was not the acquisition stock, Mr. Freeman said that it would not violate any SEC rules. "Plus," he said, "you should definitely buy our own stock."

"Buying our stock and Teledyne is a real 'no brainier,'" he added.

You thanked Bob for his advice and walked down the hall, thinking about what he had said. On the one hand, you could really use the money. You had two children ready to go to college and the bills were going to be high. On the other hand, you weren't sure if this was legal or not. It just didn't feel right. However, Bob Freeman was the CFO, so surely he would know if something of this magnitude was legal or not. All you did know was that if you did make a move to buy stock, it would have to be now.

## QUESTIONS

1. Should you buy the Texsize Oil stock and that of Teledyne?
2. Is it legal or ethical to buy either or both of these companies' stocks?
3. Should you discuss this with an attorney?
4. Should you discuss Bob Freeman's suggestion with legal counsel?
5. Does Mr. Freeman's suggestion constitute "financial advice" or is it just a comment?

# PART IX

# MANAGING THE FUTURE OF ADVERTISING


**CASE 25** **ARENDS AGENCY**
Issue: *Agency Structure*

**CASE 26** **LAWRENCEVILLE DAILY NEWS**
Issue: *Forecasting*

**CASE 27** **THOMSON MEDIA**
Issue: *FCC Media Ownership Impact*


Nobody can predict the future with perfect accuracy. However, advertising is all about understanding trends and getting aligned with them. In fact, the advertising function is one that most companies look to for a better understanding of the future.

While nobody can predict the specifics of the future, there are key areas and trends that are constantly changing. It is up to the advertising manager not only to stay abreast of these areas and trends but to put them into practice.

The areas that are under constant change in the advertising business are as follows:

- Consumer trends and behaviors.
- Media alternatives.
- Creative techniques and units.
- Research methods.
- Management practices and organization.

Consumer trends and behaviors are constantly evolving. Knowing what they are and how to research them is crucial to developing an advertising campaign. An advertising manager should devote significant time and attention to understanding what his or her customers think now and what trends might impact those beliefs in the future.

In the 1970s, the average media consideration set for a media plan was less than thirty outlets. Today, a media planner has over six hundred considerations for a plan. The number and type of media grow every day. This expansion of media also leads to new creative techniques and new creative units. All of these media outlets and creative techniques and units require consideration and some form of evaluation. Developing a solid grasp of media analysis and creative research is fundamental to good advertising.

Research methods are constantly evolving to measure the effectiveness of advertising. With the increase of behavioral data, advertisers are increasingly more able to provide specific return on investment metrics to senior management. Research is also being developed to better measure the emotional response to advertising through techniques like facial coding and neurological studies.

With new technologies coming of age, advertising organizations have greatly changed in how they work and how they are organized. There has never been only one way to organize or work, and now new theories and methods are constantly being explored.

From a high-level viewpoint, there are five broad trends impacting the advertising business.

1. Convergence: the digitalization of mass media into similar streams of data and information.
2. Interactivity: the ability of the audience to work with the media in a two-way dialogue.
3. Engagement: the involvement of a customer so that extended attention and responses can be achieved.
4. Commoditization: the increased similarity of topics, products, and content.
5. Cadence: the increased pace of change in modern life.

These five trends are greatly impacting the key areas that we discussed above: media, creative, research, management. The consumer is the one who drives all the trends. What this means is that the rules of advertising are changing and changing quickly. This is both an opportunity and a threat for managing advertising decisions.

Advertising is already a fast-paced industry. And every day the pace goes even faster. Managers must handle more responsibilities, including new challenges and shifts away from past practices and measurements. Those who can keep up will benefit as the advertising industry increases its demands for capable management.

For more information regarding managing the future of advertising, please refer to Chapters 18 and 19 in Jugenheimer and Kelley's *Advertising Management* text.

Case 25

# Arends Agency

**Issue:** *Agency Structure*

John Arends was planning a company retreat to develop a long-range plan for his advertising agency. As he looked out of his Chicago office onto Lake Michigan, he felt like a small boat on a great lake. He was the second-generation owner of the agency. His father had passed it on to him a few years earlier.

He fantasized about the days when his father was in charge of the agency and how much easier it seemed. The world had traditional media. Clients were cultivated based on friendships and employees were grateful to have a good job that was fun. Today, it just seemed that the world was in an uproar.

He had never experienced as much change as he had within the past few years. It seemed that every day a new medium or method of communication was developed. It made his head swim trying to keep up with it all. Clients were fickle and very volatile. It used to be that the client side of the business was very stable and that agencies were the ones that experienced a lot of turnover. Now, it seemed as if clients turned over quicker than the agency. He had witnessed his largest account change CMO's three times within the past two years. Just when he got one relationship under his belt, he had to start over again.

To get a handle on all of this, he told his senior leadership team that they would have a retreat and reflect on the trends that were going on in the industry and how it might impact the agency.

## Arends Agency

John's father, Dale, started the Arends Agency in 1950, after coming home from World War II. He had been a technical writer in the service and thought that there was a market for a company that understood technical selling. In a city known for big league consumer brand expertise, Dale believed that by going against the grain, he would stand out.

The agency, which began in a humble, abandoned warehouse, grew to be a strong business-to-business (B to B) agency. At its peak in 1990, the agency billed $60 million and had eighty employees. During the late 1990s and early 2000s, the Arends

Exhibit 25.1

**Arends Agency Profile, 1990 vs. Today**

| Key facts | 1990 | Today |
|---|---|---|
| Billings ($ millions) | 60.0 | 45.0 |
| # of employees | 75 | 40 |
| % B to B | 100% | 75% |

*Note*: B to B = Business to Business

Exhibit 25.2

**Key Accounts Today**

| Account | Industry |
|---|---|
| Simon Industries | Wire for cement |
| Canadian Lumber | Pulp and paper products |
| Black & Decker | Consumer tools |
| AZ Rock | Floor tiles (industrial) |
| Berwanger | Commercial glass |

Agency began to fall on hard times. The business that they had cultivated, traditional manufacturing and other industrial companies, was on the wane. John's father was reluctant to invest in other services and in technology to keep the business relevant to today's world. As a result, the agency held its current business but hadn't won any significant new business in the past few years.

John took over the agency two years ago. He saw that there was a need to invest in new resources as well as new technology. He also thought that it might be a good idea to expand the client base, and grow from a strictly business-to-business agency to one that had some consumer goods that were related to the businesses that the agency understood. For example, Arends worked for Simon Industries, the largest maker of wire for construction projects, as well as Canadian Lumber, one of the largest pulp and paper mills in the country. John used his building supply knowledge to pitch Black and Decker tools and he landed a small woodworking assignment. He hoped to do more of this, but he also knew that he needed to draft a course for the agency based on key trends in the industry.

## Industry Trends

John began gathering information on industry trends that might help him and his team with their planning session. He took at look at where the industry was in terms of revenue, where that revenue was going, and which media outlets seemed to be benefiting from it.

The U.S. advertising market always seemed to go up. However, as he looked at the numbers from the chart, he began to think that the days of double-digit growth were gone. "I imagine that the only way to experience that double-digit growth is to move to a country like India or China," he thought. Even though the U.S. advertis-

Exhibit 25.3

**U.S. Advertising Forecasts Advertising Expenditures** (millions $)

| Year | $ |
|---|---|
| 2002 | 149,756 |
| E2007 | 180,695 |
| E2008 | 188,027 |
| E2009 | 193,687 |

*Note:* E = Estimated

Exhibit 25.4 **Marketers Media Buying Expectations** (three-year forecast)

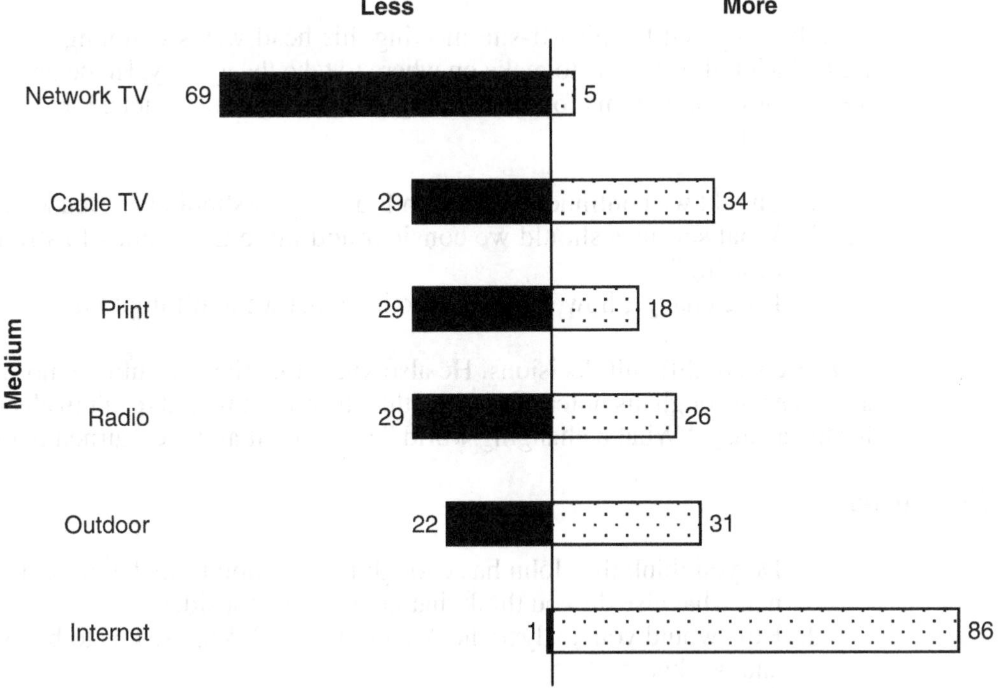


ing market was growing at a modest rate, it was still a huge market and represented nearly 50 percent of all the advertising spending in the world.

He also read that the big agency networks were diversifying well beyond advertising. In fact, he read that advertising spending accounts for less than half the $1 trillion marketing communications industry. Advertising is just one of many components in the mix. He saw that most of the advertising companies were focusing much attention on higher growth areas such as interactive media, media planning and buying, public relations, direct marketing, and customer relations management.

The changing industry environment was very much evident in the makeup of the advertising media.

John was shocked to see that spending on the Internet was already larger than that for outdoor. In fact, the Internet spending was scheduled to double from 2002 to 2009. By the year 2009, the Internet spending on advertising would approach that of the consumer magazine industry. This was just staggering to him.

He also saw that business-to-business magazine advertising was not growing at all. As a percentage of the total advertising spending, it was actually decreasing in importance. The other startling fact was that all these other media, such as mobile and alternative media, were gaining a lot of steam. It was a lot to absorb. The proliferation of new technologies such as Internet, mobile phones, wireless games, iPods, and digital video recorders was making it a challenge to keep abreast of the industry.

## Decisions for the Arends Agency

As John prepared for his off-site meeting, his head was swimming with thoughts. He had a lot of decisions to make on where to take the agency. He began to write out the key discussion items for the meeting. This is what he sketched out as an agenda for discussion.

1. Should we continue to be a B to B agency or should we broaden our scope?
2. What services should we consider adding to the agency to strengthen the offering?
3. If we change, how should we do it so that we don't implode?

These were difficult decisions. He also knew that there would be more questions as he went through his notes. He hoped that the retreat would result in clear direction for the agency. "What a changing world," he thought and then turned out the light.

## Questions

1. Do you think that John has enough information to make these decisions? If not, what else do you think that he needs to consider?
2. How would you analyze the Arends agency? What seems to be its strengths and weaknesses?
3. Based on the information in the case, what do you feel are the opportunities and threats facing the agency?
4. What would you like to know about the personnel of the Arends agency?
5. What would you like to know about their clients?

Case 26

# Lawrenceville *Daily News*

## Issue: *Forecasting*

Dale Greendale is the advertising director for the Lawrenceville *Daily News.* Lawrenceville is a Midwestern college town located more than two hundred miles from any major metropolitan area. As a result, Lawrenceville has been a bit isolated from many large metropolitan pressures.

The Lawrenceville *Daily News* is a 43,000-circulation newspaper published seven days a week. It continues to be a thriving newspaper despite the challenges to the industry from the Internet. In fact, the Lawrenceville *Daily News* has added circulation in each of the past five years, while the industry has been steadily losing ground.

Despite its stellar record, there are signs of trouble on the horizon. About ten years ago, advertising contributed 82 percent of the newspaper's total revenue. This has steadily eroded and now represents only 68 percent of total revenue.

Newspaper advertising revenue has been increasing but not as fast as other income sources. The Internet version of the paper has been successful as well and is drawing support, particularly for those advertisers who are targeting the university student population. The subscription costs for both the paper and the online product have increased so this has also added revenue to the company. In fact, during the past fiscal year, newspaper advertising revenue was up slightly at 3 percent, circulation revenue was up by 6 percent, and online revenue was up 16 percent. All of this was good news and well ahead of the industry.

However, even though revenue has been increasing, it has not kept pace with operating expenses. There are a number of issues that were very perplexing for Dale and his management.

- The actual cost for newsprint and ink was going up tremendously. Due to a paper shortage, newsprint had nearly doubled over the past six years. Every time they printed the paper, it cost them more and more.
- The Lawrenceville *Daily News* had developed a staff for the newspaper and a staff for the online version of the newspaper. They had separate advertising departments and editorial and production departments. It seemed that neither the newspaper staff nor the online staff wanted to mix with each other. Not

Exhibit 26.1

**Lawrenceville *Daily News* Revenue Sources**

| Item | Total $(000) | % Total | % Increase vs. Year Ago |
|---|---|---|---|
| Newspaper Advertising | 34,000 | 68 | 3 |
| Online Advertising | 8,500 | 17 | 16 |
| Circulation (both online and print) | 7,500 | 15 | 6 |
| Total | 50,000 | 100 | 6 |

Exhibit 26.2

**Lawrenceville *Daily News* Operating Expenses, Cost vs. Year Ago** (in %)

| Item | % Increase vs. Year Ago |
|---|---|
| Operational | |
| Newsprint/Ink | 16 |
| Press Room | 7 |
| Composing | 6 |
| IT Bandwidth | 10 |
| IT General Expenses | 12 |
| Circulation Expenses | 10 |
| Marketing Expenses | 10 |
| Building | 3 |
| Personnel | |
| Advertising Sales | 11 |
| Editorial | 20 |
| Interactive Production | 18 |
| Employee Benefits | 15 |

*Note*: IT = Information Technology

only were they separated by delivery method, they were miles apart in terms of philosophy.

- Healthcare coverage was a big expense. Lawrenceville *Daily News* was a family-owned business. In fact, Dale's uncle, Earl Greendale, was the publisher. Dale knew from conversations with Earl that they had one of the best healthcare programs in the country but the costs were going through the roof. Earl had told Dale that he was very concerned that he would have to cut employee benefits to continue to fund the operation.

The last subscription rate increase took effect about fourteen months ago. The single-copy price was raised as was the online subscription price. Dale began to see that they were reaching a ceiling on pricing of both the newspaper and online products. Circulation was growing but only because Lawrenceville's population was growing at a rate of 6 percent a year. However, once the rate increase had taken effect, Dale saw that circulation was growing at only 2 percent a year. The online product, which had been growing at a double-digit rate, was now growing only about 5 percent.

Not only did they increase the subscription rate to the consumer, they increased the rates for the advertisers as well within the same time frame. A rate increase of 6 percent was passed on to the advertisers for both the print and the online products. It accounted for a lot of the growth in total revenue but Dale was worried that all they were doing was increasing costs for their current customers. All of these rate hikes are not attracting new customers to our product even though we are in a growth market.

Dale was asked by his uncle Earl to develop a plan to meet this challenge. As Earl told him, "You can either raise the bridge or lower the water." That was Earl's way of saying that you either had to bring in more revenue or cut some costs. Dale replied, "It sounds simple when you put it like that." But, Dale knew that it wasn't so simple. Every area was very complex and by impacting one of the areas, there was a ripple effect throughout the organization.

Time was of the essence, so Dale began to draft a plan for the future.

## QUESTIONS

1. What should Dale's plan contain?
2. Do you think that Dale should tackle costs first and then growth or do it the other way around?
3. What changes do you think would have the greatest long-term impact on the business?
4. Should Dale consult with other companies before he does his plan?
5. What other items should Dale consider before he does his plan?

Case 27

# Thomson Media

## Issue: *FCC Media Ownership Impact*

Jim Thomson, CEO of Thomson Media, felt that he had got the ball rolling. His family was the majority owner of Thomson Media, now one of the top media conglomerates in the United States.

Mr. Thomson had been pressured to consider the sale of Thomson Media to a real-estate mogul, Herbert Zellman. However, Mr. Zellman was not interested in the company unless the Federal Communications Commission (FCC) showed some signs of loosening its restrictions on market-level ownership of multiple media properties.

In the past six months, Mr. Thomson had lobbied the FCC to ease its restrictions so that they could sell their company to Mr. Zellman. Mr. Thomson felt that he was pushing the FCC to make some significant changes. He had personally established a rapport with the head of the FCC, Kevin Brown. He had made countless trips to Washington, D.C., to lobby on behalf of loosening the restrictions.

The announcement in the local paper's business section that day was as follows: "After years of debate, the head of the Federal Communications Commission proposed a relatively modest change in media-ownership rules that appeared tailored to ensure the completion of the Thomson Media deal with real-estate magnate, Herbert Zellman."

The article went on to say that Kevin Brown, the head of the FCC, wants to allow a company to own both one newspaper and a radio or television station in the top 20 media markets—subject to certain conditions. The proposal fell short of scrapping the thirty-two-year-old ban on cross-media ownership. Plus even this small change was sure to trigger further discussion within the five-member commission.

The proposal was welcome news for Thomson Media, which owns newspapers and television stations in four markets and has waivers from the ban. The four markets of Chicago, Los Angeles, Miami, and New York are among the largest in the country. If the commission approves Mr. Brown's plan, a major obstacle would be removed to the multibillion deal with Mr. Zellman, who would otherwise have to get the waivers renewed. This was not a likely scenario.

Only in Roanoke, Virginia, where Thomson Media owns the Roanoke *Gazette* newspaper and two television stations, is there a potential problem. If Mr. Brown's proposal is adopted, Thomson Media would have to apply for a waiver or sell assets in that market.

Under Mr. Brown's proposal, there would have to be at least eight other "media voices" in that market, including newspapers and major commercial television stations, and the television station couldn't be one of the four largest channels in the market.

The Thomson Media Company met all of these criteria in the four large markets where it owns both newspapers and television stations. Unfortunately, the television stations in Roanoke were the top two in the market so they didn't meet the criteria in this smaller market.

While Mr. Thomson was pleased that some action had been taken by the FCC, he wasn't totally satisfied with the outcome. He wanted to put more pressure on the FCC to totally expand the ownership so that he would have no roadblocks in selling the company. He released a statement to the press saying, "Thomson Media would seek an expansion of cross-ownership relief within the next few weeks."

A spokesperson for Mr. Zellman declined to comment on the FCC proceedings but a person close to him said that Mr. Zellman was eager to get the Thomson Media deal done by the end of the year and would be pleased if the FCC gave in on the top Thomson Media markets. Also, if the deal isn't closed by the end of the year, Mr. Zellman would have to pay a fee to help Thomson Media with their taxes.

Mr. Brown's plan didn't go exactly as many people expected, but Mr. Brown felt that it was necessary to begin with some progress rather than try for significant reforms that may or may not be approved by the committee. Even with this reform, he knew that he was being scrutinized due to the Thomson Media situation.

Mr. Brown released a statement saying that his plan wasn't "directly related to any particular sale." He went on to say that the rule changes that he proposed would preserve the vitality of newspapers by allowing them to share their operational costs across multiple media platforms.

Still, certain members of Congress were not ready for these reforms. They felt that they hurt the public by consolidating media voices. One public interest group, Freedom of the Press, indicated that his group and others would challenge the ruling in court if it passed.

Mr. Thomson knew that there was some pressure on Mr. Zellman to close out the deal, but he also knew that unless Mr. Zellman felt certain that the FCC would deliver Brown's plan that there would be no deal.

Mr. Thomson called a meeting of the board. He said, "We have got Kevin Brown on our side even though he didn't go all the way for us. Now we need to make sure that the rest of the committee votes for this and that we don't have outside congressional or political distractions. Let's develop a plan to get it done now."

## QUESTIONS

1. What should Mr. Thomson plan be?
2. What methods do you think that Mr. Thomson should take to ensure that the FCC approves Mr. Brown's plan?
3. Do you feel that Mr. Brown was acting on the best interest of the country with his proposal?
4. If you were Mr. Zellman, would you commit to buying Thomson Media based on the current FCC proposal?

# PART X

# MANAGING YOURSELF

**CASE 28 STATE UNIVERSITY**
**Issue:** *Advertising Instruction Ethics*

**CASE 29 KMF AGENCY**
**ISSUE:** *Ethical Issue of When to Change Jobs*

**CASE 30 GOTHAM MEDIA**
**Issue:** *New Job Responsibilities*

Most advertising managers are so busy managing either people, processes, or the advertising product that they rarely stop to think about how best they should work and what they are working toward. You are only as good as you make yourself. There are keys to becoming successful in the advertising business.

The largest key to success is to properly manage time. Time is your most important asset. We all have the same amount of time: 168 hours a week. But some persons get much more accomplished than others during this time.

Time management is especially important in advertising, because time is all you have to sell. We know that you are really selling ideas, plans, campaigns, and counsel, but they all involve time. How you use your time determines the success or failure of the organization and the advertising product.

Most people waste as much as 80 percent of their time. The top five timewasters for mangers are:

1. Doing work beneath your capabilities.
2. Tolerating too many interruptions.
3. Handling trivial assignments while delaying the big project.
4. Working without a plan.
5. Saying "yes" too much.

The key to gaining control over your time is to have a plan, properly delegate responsibility, schedule meetings and also quiet time, and constantly take in feedback on what works and what doesn't.

There are many time management systems and techniques used in management today. Explore what works for you. You will need to learn to multitask. The advertising business demands that you work quickly and on multiple projects at once. This may seem daunting at first, but advertising managers all develop personal systems to cope with the steady steam of decisions that need to be made.

If you can manage an advertising campaign or an advertising department or an advertising agency, you should also be able to manage your own career. Think of yourself as a brand or a product. Are you gaining position in the marketplace or just holding your own? What is your vision for your brand? Does the reality of what you are doing right now help you achieve that vision?

Your career is like a product. You need to promise a benefit and have some unique characteristics that make people think of you and prefer you. Hopefully, you will build enough brand assets that people will be willing to pay a premium price for your service. After all, you don't want to be the Wal-Mart of the advertising business, do you?

While an employer may help train you to do specific tasks, do not expect anyone else to help manage your career. You may find mentors along the way that take an interest in you but at the end of the day, where you go is largely up to you. So, plot a course and constantly revisit your goals to see if you are making progress.

Most of us have specific criteria for success. It may be to make a certain salary, buy a new house, travel extensively, or retire when you are forty. Most goals revolve around money. However, we caution you to not measure your career success solely on money.

Sure, money is important. However, many things in life are not material. Managing your career is just one part of managing to live a successful life. So, when you evaluate your own career success, take into account such things as work ethic, your habits, and your influence on other people. And don't forget your personal life, your relationships, and how other people think of you.

For more information on managing yourself, please refer to Chapters 20 and 21 in the Jugenheimer and Kelley's *Advertising Management* textbook.

Case 28

# State University

## ISSUE: *Advertising Instruction Ethics*

Dr. Edward Johnson had never resolved his personal dilemma about teaching advertising. Dr. Johnson was the head of the advertising program at a large state university. He had grown the program from a few courses in the School of Communications to an entire Department of Advertising.

Throughout his teaching, he had always told a story that was very positive about the role of advertising in the economy, how much fun it was as a profession, and how there were career opportunities in it for those who wanted to pursue it aggressively.

Students flocked to the advertising program. They found it to be a fascinating area. They enjoyed hearing about the strategies behind familiar advertising campaigns and debated the virtues of advertising to children and other societal issues concerning paid communications. For the most part, students left the initial class in advertising, "Survey of Advertising," with most of their stereotypes in tact. These included the ideas that advertising was a glamorous field and that it had a positive impact on society as a general rule.

Dr. Johnson was a great teacher and had such a positive attitude that he attracted many students to the "Survey of Advertising" class. It was one of the most popular classes on campus. The latest figures showed that this class (split into three sections) alone attracted over six hundred students. More than 90 percent of these students went on to declare themselves advertising majors. More advertising majors led to more interdepartmental budget clout since student credit hours translated to revenue for the school. This then led to better faculty salaries and more resources for the Advertising Department. All of this was a positive for Dr. Johnson and the School of Communications itself.

However, Dr. Johnson knew that there were other aspects of advertising that he didn't play up. It wasn't that he ignored them; it was just that he didn't emphasize them.

The first was that there was a lot of criticism of advertising and the role it played in our society.

One critic said, "National advertising serves primarily to artificially differentiate parity products and actually inhibits existing and potential competition."

Another critic said that advertising has too much sway in media and cited a number of cases where advertisers helped to shape editorial policies at various media companies.

Dr. Johnson did touch upon some of this material in passing but it was more in the vein of "look at what some of the critics have to say about advertising." Usually, he dismissed it with the saying: "Advertising encourages—not discourages—competition."

The second area was that advertising did not provide a working environment of positive growth. Many advertising professionals said that advertising is a business and that it was not a place for the meek.

Justin Marks, an agency principal said, "The only real reason to go into advertising is that you enjoy solving problems and making money. We aren't serving humanity here; we are trying to help clients sell their goods."

Anthropologist Bobbi Freeman, who had spent ten years in an agency as an account planner said, "If you are kind, gentle, ethical, or religious then advertising is not the place for you. Advertising requires strong defenses, toughness, nerves of steel, and the willingness to exploit oneself and others."

Jennifer Stevens, a former copywriter said, "This is not a game about developing witty and catchy headlines. The advertising business is about cold, hard-nosed businessmen who happen to have your number."

Dr. Johnson wanted to present a fair and balanced viewpoint of the advertising business but he also knew that if he presented all this material on the ups and downs of the business that he couldn't get to other material that the students found fun and exciting. Plus the tone of the class would become more somber and Dr. Johnson thought that the more negative the viewpoint, the more likely it was that students would not pursue advertising as a major.

The final item that Dr. Johnson didn't bring up was the statistics on where advertising majors went after college. Dr. Johnson did have some star former students who had made their mark in the creative departments of large New York and Chicago advertising agencies. In fact, Dr. Johnson brought in many of his former pupils to sing the praises of advertising and to foster the dream of a creative career.

Most students who came into advertising had dreams of being the next great copywriter or creative director at a Madison Avenue agency. However, the truth was that less than 10 percent of advertising majors went on to be copywriters in any agency or company. Less than 2 percent went on to be copywriters at top 100 agencies in the country. The majority of advertising majors went into other areas of advertising such as media or account management. However, the majority of advertising majors eventually ended up in areas outside of advertising such as retail management or sales.

Dr. Johnson never shared these statistics with the students. He did not hide that it was difficult to make it in the advertising business but he did not publish any statistics on the success rate even though he kept a good database of former advertising students.

So, Dr. Johnson felt conflicted. On the one hand, he knew that enrollment was the key to academic success and the well-being of his colleagues. On the other hand, he did have an obligation to the students to tell them the truth about the field.

Of course, he knew that students would get other views of advertising in other courses outside of the department, so he didn't feel that it was totally his responsibility to tell all sides of the story. His role was to build a strong department.

"So, perhaps it's best not to mess with success," Dr. Johnson thought. He did say to himself that he would try to add more controversial material to the "Survey of Advertising" course if he could find the time to fit it in.

## QUESTIONS

1. Should Dr. Johnson change the way he is teaching the "Survey of Advertising" class?
2. What obligations does the Department of Advertising have regarding the sharing of information with students?
3. Should Dr. Johnson's priority be to build the largest and strongest Department of Advertising?
4. Should Dr. Johnson always provide both pros and cons of each situation?
5. Do you think that the negatives would impact students from studying advertising?

# Case 29 KMF Agency

## Issue: *Ethical Issue of When to Change Jobs*

Sarah Rasmussen felt like she had it made. Her hard work in school was paying off. Sarah was a recent graduate of a top-tier advertising program. She had maintained a 3.5 GPA and she was actively involved in all the advertising clubs in her school. She had been the Account Director of her AAF Campaigns class competition. She was proud that their school finished in the top two in their district and had the opportunity to go to nationals. While they didn't place at the national competition, the experience was great.

Her professor had encouraged her to apply for a scholarship that was awarded by a large advertising agency in Dallas. The scholarship not only helped defray her school costs but it came with a paid internship at the advertising agency. The agency, KMF, was a large independent agency in the Southwest. KMF was a venerable old agency that was in the midst of retooling itself to meet the new digital age. KMF management hoped that this scholarship would not only be a good thing to do but that it would also help the agency attract new talent to meet the new age of advertising.

Sarah won the scholarship, beating out twenty other candidates from around the Southwest. She and her professor were flown to Dallas, where the agency awarded the scholarship at an Advertising Club function. KMF also paid for her parents to be there; flying them in from Odessa, Texas. Sarah's parents and her professor were very proud of Sarah. They were also very impressed with the first-class way that KMF had treated them and her.

Sarah was allowed to participate in one of KMF's largest accounts: a large computer manufacturer. Sarah got to meet the client and sat in on strategy sessions. KMF also trained her in the way the agency operated. The last week of her internship, KMF offered Sarah a full-time position with the agency, working in the same account group that she had interned with.

"Sarah, this is a great opportunity for you to contribute to the agency. We are excited about having you as one of the new generation of KMF associates to help us in this new digital age," said the KMF account director, Alice Woods.

Sarah really liked KMF. They were very professional yet very family oriented. It fit her strong family background. The agency's advertising accounts reflected the agency's personality. They handled a number of large corporations and did very professional yet very conservative work. The only downside of KMF was that it didn't have a lot of people her age in the agency. Most of the KMF associates had been with the company for a long time. As a result, most of them were at least ten years older than she was and many were her parents' age. She missed having people to socialize with after work. But, she did have friends from school who had relocated to Dallas; so it wasn't that hard to find people to do things with. Plus, if she wanted to go home and see her parents; it was only a five-hour drive or, better yet, a quick thirty-minute plane trip.

Sarah had been at her job for six months when she got a call from Debbie Tippen, one of her teammates on the AAF competition team. Debbie had graduated before Sarah and was working for a very hot creative agency in Miami, The Hot House. Sarah had visited Debbie in Miami over spring break. While in Miami, Debbie arranged for Sarah to have a courtesy interview with Keith Manheim, one of the founders of The Hot House. Keith told her that The Hot House was all about creativity and that digital media would be the center of the new advertising universe.

Keith showed Sarah around the agency. It was set up like a youth hostel. There were beanbag chairs everywhere and even bunk beds. They had rooms with big-screen televisions that were playing music videos. Everyone in the agency had laptop computers so that they could work anywhere and everywhere that they wanted. Sarah thought it was really cool. The Hot House was doing some cutting-edge work. Most of their accounts were youth-oriented brands such as shoes, soft drinks, beer and wine, and ski equipment.

A week later, Debbie called Sarah: "Keith Manheim wanted me to tell you that he has a job for you at The Hot House. It's on Silver, the new fashion company that is coming to the U.S. from France." Debbie went on to tell Sarah that she would have to go to Paris every other month to meet with the client's foreign marketing director.

"Keith remembered that you can speak French and told me to call you right away. I have a place for you on the beach. We can be a team again just like we were in college. The work here is awesome and the people are just too cool," said Debbie.

Sarah said, "But Debbie, I have a good job and have only been on it for six months. It sounds great but I don't know that it would be right to leave."

Debbie replied, "Sarah, are you nuts! The Hot House is up for creative agency of the year. You get to go to Paris for free and live on the beach. Isn't that a lot better than doing that stodgy agency thing in Dallas? Plus, I haven't seen many beaches too close to Dallas." Debbie then said that Sarah should at least call Keith and discuss the job with him.

"It never hurts to talk," said Debbie.

Sarah reluctantly did call Keith Manheim. Keith quickly began to convince Sarah that this was a job of a lifetime.

"Look, Sarah, you were meant for this job and for this agency. Your background is perfect for this account. I think that it will be the next great cosmetics company in the U.S. The client is awesome and wants to do work that will win Clios. Plus, I will pay you 20 percent more than you are making now. Let me know by Friday and let's make it happen," said Keith.

Sarah hung up the phone and looked at her computer screen. "What should I do," she thought.

## QUESTIONS

1. Should Sarah take the job at The Hot House?
2. Should Sarah discuss the job offer with KMF?
3. If Sarah decides to leave, should she give back the scholarship money?
4. If Sarah stays, should she ask for a 20 percent raise?
5. How long should you stay at your first job?

# Case 30 Gotham Media

## Issue: *New Job Responsibilities*

Kyle Bennett had very high standards. Kyle was a rising star in the media department of Gotham Media, one of the top media planning and buying companies in the United States.

Kyle had joined the firm just two years ago, out of college. Within that time, he had been promoted twice from an assistant to a media planner and most recently to a media supervisor. The last transition had been the hardest for Kyle. Kyle was used to doing everything himself. As an assistant, he took on work that no one else wanted to do. He plowed through paperwork and became known in the company as one of the few assistants who actually cared about his work.

Kyle knew if he worked hard, he would get ahead. He was right. His promotion to media planner happened within the first six months on the job. As a media planner, he was responsible for helping his supervisor develop media plans and then coordinate the execution of those plans. Within three months, his supervisor had basically turned over the smaller accounts to Kyle to run with. This suited Kyle's style and he periodically checked in with his supervisor but did the work himself. He loved making it happen and really enjoyed seeing the project through.

His only frustration was in executing the media plans. There he lost some control since he basically developed the media buying specifications and then turned it over to other buying teams to execute the plan. Gotham Media was set up with specialists who purchased each medium from network television to print to online media. Kyle's job was to give them the purchase parameters and then to follow up to make sure they did their job.

Kyle had a few run-ins with some of the buying supervisors, since he rejected some of the media buys as not meeting his purchase specifications. In fact, for one outdoor purchase, he asked the out-of-home buying supervisor if he could do it himself. She gave him the "go ahead" and Kyle did the outdoor buy himself.

While the senior management of Gotham Media thought Kyle was a bit headstrong, they also thought that he was a rapidly rising media star.

"There just aren't too many young adults who throw themselves into a job with such passion as Kyle," said one of the senior Gotham managers.

Kyle's immediate supervisor agreed and said, "Kyle is a quick study. He gets it done and done right. He is quite a perfectionist—which can be a good thing and a bad thing."

Based on Kyle's stellar performance as a media planner, he was promoted to a media supervisor. While others in the company recognized that Kyle was a rising star, it did rankle some veterans that he was being promoted so fast.

"It is one thing to be a great media planner and another to be a supervisor of people," said one of the older associate media directors.

Kyle was in charge of a group of twelve accounts, three media planners, and two assistant planners. Two of the media planners were roughly Kyle's age and one was ten years older. They were assigned to work on four accounts apiece and the assistants were there to support the entire group.

Kyle knew that the planners weren't as good as he was and he was concerned that the quality of work would suffer as a result. He decided that he should take a hand in every media plan that came out of his group. He began to work with each planner on plans but soon found himself doing the plans on his own. He found that it was easier to write them the way he felt was best, as opposed to letting the planners work them and then have them continually rewrite them the way he wanted.

However, by taking on twelve accounts compared to the four he had as a planner was proving to be a difficult task. He was working fourteen-hour days and still had trouble getting his work done. He also saw that the media execution was slipping. This was due to the fact that the media planners didn't know what the plans were about, since Kyle was doing them all and not involving them in the process.

Julie Jones, one of the media planners around Kyle's age said, "Kyle, I want to help you but if you don't tell me what is going on, it is impossible for me to help the buying groups execute the plans."

Kyle was struggling and he was particularly frustrated with Mary Redmond, a thirty-four-year-old planner who had been in the same position for ten years. He found it incredible that someone had stayed in the same position for that long, and had disdain for her.

However, Mary handled a tedious job of coordinating a multimarket retailer who had nearly daily changes in their newspaper schedule. Mary liked the account and knew that she made a good contribution to the company. She had been offered promotions but said that she preferred to be a planner on this account since she could have some flexibility to pick up her kids from school. "If I was a supervisor, I would have to deal with a lot more issues and it wouldn't be fair to my family," she said.

Kyle had tried to change things on this retail account to no avail. He thought that the retailer was missing an opportunity by not using media other than print. But, in meeting after meeting, the retail client said that he was happy with print. It was working and until he felt that it didn't work; he was going to continue on this course.

Kyle was really frustrated with his group's performance and with his lack of time to make it all happen. He felt that the group wasn't pushing clients ahead fast enough and he was frustrated that he couldn't ensure that everything was done his way.

"I just don't have time to train this group so I guess I will have to work harder to make it happen," thought Kyle. He also wondered how long he could keep working at this pace. The long hours were taking its toll on him and everyone else around him.

Finally, one day, his associate media director called Kyle into his office. "Kyle, we need to talk," he said.

## QUESTIONS

1. What advice do you think that Kyle's associate media director gave him?
2. How can Kyle get more control of his time?
3. What sacrifices will Kyle have to make to become a better supervisor?
4. How do you deal with people like Mary, who have career goals that are very different from your own?
5. What would you say to Kyle if you had been a media planner in his group?
6. Have you ever been on a team where the star tries to do too much? What happened?

# About the Authors

**Larry Kelley** is Executive Vice President, Chief Planning Officer for FKM, the sixtieth largest advertising agency in the United States, where he is also an agency principal. Since joining FogartyKleinMonroe, now FKM, in 1990, Kelley has held senior roles in media, account planning, and interactive. Prior to joining FogartyKleinMonroe in 1990, Mr. Kelley served in senior media and research positions with BBD&O, Bozell & Jacobs, and the Bloom Agency.

Mr. Kelley has worked on a wide variety of clients and categories for both domestic and international companies. He has worked with such firms as American Airlines, ConAgra Foods, Conoco/Phillips, Dell, Georgia-Pacific, Kroger, Minute Maid, Southwestern Bell, Yum Brands, and Zales.

He has also written or cowritten six books on advertising as well as a popular culture book. He has been awarded with four EFFIES for advertising effectiveness and has won ADDY awards. Mr. Kelley is also a Professor of Advertising at the University of Houston, where he heads the advertising sequence in the Jack J. Valenti School of Communications. He also serves on numerous boards for private industry as well as the 4A's media council.

Mr. Kelley holds a B.S. in journalism from the University of Kansas and a Master's Degree in Advertising from the University of Texas at Austin.

**Dr. Donald W. Jugenheimer** is an author, researcher, consultant, and educator. His specialties are advertising and media management, media economics, and advertising media.

As a consultant, Dr. Jugenheimer has worked with such firms as American Airlines, IBM, Century 21 real estate, Aetna Insurance, Pacific Telesis, and the U.S. Army Recruiting Command, and he currently consults on a variety of research and advisory projects in advertising and marketing, including advertising media plans for class-action lawsuits. He has also conducted research for a variety of enterprises including for the U.S. Department of Health, Education and Welfare, for the International Association of Business Communicators, and for National Liberty Life Insurance.

Dr. Jugenheimer is author or coauthor of eighteen books and many articles and papers. He has spoken before a variety of academic and professional organizations, including the World Advertising Congress in Tokyo. He also served as President and as Executive Director of the American Academy of Advertising and as Advertising Division Head of the Association for Education in Journalism and Mass Communication. He also was Business Manager for the founding of the *Journal of Advertising.*

He has testified about advertising before the U.S. House of Representatives Armed Forces Committee as well as in federal and state court proceedings.

Since earning his PhD in Communications from the University of Illinois with a specialization in advertising and a minor in marketing, Dr. Jugenheimer has been a tenured member of the faculties at the University of Kansas, Louisiana State University (where he was the first person to hold the Manship Distinguished Professorship in Journalism), Fairleigh Dickinson University, Southern Illinois University, and Texas Tech University. At most of those universities, he also served as an administrator. His bachelor's degree was in advertising with a minor in economics and his master's degree was also in advertising with a minor in marketing. All three degrees are from the University of Illinois at Urbana-Champaign. He worked at several adverting agencies in Chicago and downstate Illinois. He also served in the U.S. Air Force, first in aeromedical evacuation and later as a medical administrative officer.

Dr. Jugenheimer has lectured and conducted workshops in several countries and served on the guest faculty of the Executive Media MBA program for the Turku School of Economics and Business Administration in Finland. In addition, he has held a Kellogg National Fellowship. He is listed in *Who's Who in America, Who's Who in Advertising, Who's Who in Education,* and several other biographical references.

Dr. Jugenheimer is currently a partner and principal in the research, writing, and consulting firm In-Telligence.